DECEIVED
by the
LIGHT

DOUG GROOTHUIS

HARVEST HOUSE PUBLISHERS
Eugene, Oregon 97402

DECEIVED BY THE LIGHT

Copyright © 1995 by Harvest House Publishers
Eugene, Oregon 97402

Library of Congress Cataloging-in-Publication Data

Groothuis, Doug R., 1957–
    Deceived by the light : a biblical response to mega-bestseller Embraced by the light / Doug Groothuis.
        p.   cm.
    ISBN 1-56507-301-0
    1. Eadie, Betty J. (Betty Jean), 1942. Embraced by the light. 2. Near-death experiences. 3. Near-death experiences—Religious aspects—Christianity. I. Title.
BF1045.N4E23   1995   95-5157
133.9′01′3—dc20   CIP

Printed in the United States of America.

95 96 97 98 99 00 01 02 — 10 9 8 7 6 5 4 3 2

To my beloved Becky,
   for her wit,
   insight,
   intelligence,
 · faithfulness, and
      love.

You are a light
   from
      the Light

ACKNOWLEDGMENTS

This project was born when Ken Myers, of Mars Hill Audio, interviewed me about Betty Eadie's book *Embraced by the Light*. Charles Strohmer provided substantive editorial assistance early on and contributed much to the section on Betty Eadie's account of her death. His hard work and insights improved the book considerably.

Rebecca Merrill Groothuis, my wife, did further rewriting and editing in order to help meet the pressing deadline. She also contributed significantly to several sections of the book. All this despite the fact that she had just finished a book manuscript of her own and needed a break! Becky was very much a collaborator in this entire venture; her intellectual and spiritual assistance were indispensible—again.

Dr. Kenneth Ring was a more-than-obliging correspondent concerning aspects of this project—answering questions, providing materials, and reviewing portions of the manuscript on naturalistic explanations of the near-death experience. Although our worldviews and interpretations of the near-death experience differ radically, I appreciate his interaction with me.

I am also thankful to Pastor Manny Martinez of Barnabas International for arranging a meeting with Bob and Debbie Bierma, whose story of their daughter I recount in chapter 2. The Biermas shared their tragedy with me, a stranger, in the hope that it might warn others about the kind of spiritual deception to which their daughter fell prey. I am deeply thankful for their courage and willingness to help.

Finally, I am grateful for the enthusiasm and encouragement of my publisher, Harvest House. They believed in the book, got behind it, and were patient when it took longer to write than originally anticipated.

CONTENTS

DECEIVED
by the
LIGHT

1

BETTY AND THE LIGHT

I'm not afraid of death. I just don't want to be there when it happens.

—Woody Allen

Death is not our friend. It is an unwanted companion that we do our best to ignore. We push it out of sight and out of mind—on the obituary page in the back of the newspaper and in secluded graveyards we call "resting places." The absolute sense of finality proves too much for us to bear. Yet it is this very inevitability and finality that forces us to find ways to live with the reality of death.

> We know that we will die, and that knowledge invades our consciousness, shapes our artifacts, arts, and sciences; it will not let us rest until we have found ways, through rituals and stories, theologies and philosophies, either to make sense of death or, failing that, to make sense of ourselves in the face of death.[1]

The unending effort to come to terms with death distinguishes humans from animals. Throughout history, people in every society have memorialized the demise of their fellows by performing solemn rituals, by ceremonially preparing and burying the remains, and by searching out the mystery of death in the hope of finding its meaning.

Dealing with death is not an optional activity, as the philosopher Blaise Pascal ruthlessly illustrates:

> Imagine a number of men in chains, all under sentence of death, some of whom are each day butchered in the sight of all the others; those remaining see their own condition in that of their fellows, and looking at each other with grief and despair await their turn. This is an image of the human condition.[2]

Unless we find some meaning to death, we will see no meaning to life; for our lives are permeated by death.

Recently, this ongoing human need has been expressed in a number of popular accounts that seek not to *evade* the reality of death but to *redefine* it. Increasing numbers of people are proclaiming that death is not the end, that it is nothing to fear, that there is no hell to avoid, and that death is simply another stage in one's spiritual development. These death-defying assertions are not based on any sacred Scripture, but on the testimonies of people who claim to have been clinically dead for a short time and to have experienced visions of a world beyond—a world of intense light and love.

A BESTSELLER IS BORN

Several recent bestsellers on near-death experiences (NDEs) enthusiastically declare the desirability of the world beyond. Of all these books, Betty Eadie's *Embraced by the Light* (1992) is probably the most popular, having had a long run as a *New York Times* number-one bestseller.

Embraced by the Light differs from many popular books on the subject in that it is not a study of the NDE phenomenon but simply a firsthand report of Betty Eadie's alleged near-death experience and the events related to it. Eadie was encouraged to write the book after she had spoken about her experience at churches and other gatherings in the late 1980s. Curtis Taylor, a Utah-based book editor, was so enthusiastic about the project that he became her coauthor and publisher. And what a bonanza it was!

The initial printing of 20,000 copies sold in two weeks and the second printing of 30,000 also went quickly. Within six months the book was on the *New York Times* bestseller list, where it stayed for well over a year, selling more than a million copies. Paperback rights for the book were sold for nearly two million dollars, after which the paperback edition zoomed to the bestseller lists as well. And at the time of this writing, Eadie is busy speaking around the country and writing another book.

The dust jacket claims that the book offers "astonishing proof of a life after physical death," and that Eadie "saw more, perhaps, than any other person has seen before, and she came back with an almost photographic view." Her story is endorsed by the prominent NDE researcher and medical doctor Melvin Morse, author of two NDE bestsellers, *Closer to the Light* (1990) and *Transformed by the Light* (1992). Morse declares that Eadie's book is a world-class revelation:

> There is a great secret contained in *Embraced by the Light*. It is a secret that you already know. It is something that the great prophets and spiritual leaders have tried to tell us for thousands of years. Betty Eadie learned it by nearly dying. It has the power to change your life.[3]

Clearly, *Embraced by the Light* has tapped into a tremendous human desire to find peace, fulfillment, and freedom from fear. In *People* magazine Eadie said, "People are in pain. They've lost hope, they're confused and desperately fear death." But she offered reassurance. "After you've died, what else is there to fear? No love can compare with the unconditional love I was shown." This was quite an about-face for Eadie. "Before dying," she said, "I thought I'd go straight to hell."[4]

Eadie's clearest message is that there is nothing to fear. Beyond death's door awaits a glorious light, full of unconditional love and acceptance for everyone who crosses that threshold. Therein lies our eternal destiny, our joy, our home—the place that we belong. To our deepest dread, Eadie offers solace; to our deepest yearning, she extends a bright promise of fulfillment.

C.S. Lewis spoke of "the inconsolable secret" that is in each of us, that "desire for our own far-off country, . . . for something that has never actually appeared in our experience."[5] We have "the sense that in this universe we are treated as strangers." We long "to be acknowledged, to meet with some response, to bridge some chasm that yawns between us and reality, . . . to be reunited with something in the universe from which we now feel cut off, to be on the inside of some door which we have always seen from the outside." We yearn for a "welcome into the heart of things."[6]

If, indeed, *this* is what we all want more than anything else, then what could be marketed with more success than a story that tells us this glorious destiny is already ours at no cost? We want so badly for it to be true that the temptation is to believe the story instinctively even if it is inconclusive and unverifiable. Its language is fascinating and appealing, and we believe it.

Consider how Betty Eadie tells her story:

> I saw a pinpoint of light in the distance. The black
> mass around me began to take on more of the shape

of a tunnel, and I felt myself traveling through it at an even greater speed, rushing toward the light. I was instinctively attracted to it. . . . As I approached it, I noticed the figure of a man standing in it, with the light radiating all around him. . . . I saw that the light immediately around him was golden, as if his whole body had a golden halo around it, and I could see that the golden halo burst out from around him and spread into a brilliant, magnificent whiteness that extended out for some distance. I felt his light blending into mine, literally, and I felt my light being drawn to his. . . . And as our lights merged, I felt as if I had stepped into his countenance, and I felt an utter explosion of love. It was the most unconditional love I have ever felt, and as I saw his arms open to receive me I went to him and received his complete embrace and said over and over, "I'm home. I'm home. I'm finally home." I felt his enormous spirit and knew that I had always been a part of him, that in reality I had never been away from him. . . . There was no questioning who he was. I knew that he was my Savior, and friend, and God. He was Jesus Christ.[7]

This certainly is attractive, but it calls for a dose of healthy skepticism. In view of what is at stake—the eternal state of one's soul—a number of significant questions need to be asked. Because Eadie's Jesus doesn't simply embrace her but teaches her about the nature of God, humanity, death, and the afterlife, it is especially important that her report be scrutinized.

Who is Eadie's Jesus? Is he the Jesus of the New Testament? What is this Jesus teaching? Does it square with the Bible? Who are the beings Eadie calls "monks," who act as her spirit guides? Is Eadie's spirituality Mormon, Gnostic, Platonic, New

Age, or Christian—or some combination of these? Did she really die in 1973, as she claims? And what about the claims of other bestsellers about the near-death experience, which seem to lend weight to Eadie's story? Let's begin our inquiry with Betty Eadie herself.

HER LIFE

Before we explore her near-death experience, it is important to understand Eadie's background, especially since her views of God and the afterlife would so greatly change after her experience.

Eadie claims that at age four she was diagnosed as having whooping cough and double pneumonia. She remembers hearing the doctor's words in the hospital, "It's too late; we've lost her," and feeling the covers being pulled over her head. She remembers the room brightening and finding herself in the calming arms of a man who had a sparkling white beard. This peaceful scene was shattered when she heard a nurse call out, "She's breathing again!" She recovered and asked her parents about the man with the beautiful beard, but they had no answers.[8] (This strange experience is but a shadow of what she reports about her 1973 NDE.)

Eadie had a rough life—one without security or religious certainty. One of ten children, she was raised on the Rosebud Reservation in South Dakota. Her parents separated when she was four, and she was placed in a strict Roman Catholic boarding school where she says she was belittled for being half Sioux and was taught a harsh, unloving view of God, which frightened her terribly. God "seemed angry and impatient and very powerful, which meant that he would probably destroy me or send me straight to hell on Judgment Day—or before if I crossed him. This boarding-school god was a being I hoped never to meet."[9]

She later was moved to a Methodist school and learned about "a happier God who was pleased when we were happy." But she "remained convinced that he was still the God who would punish me if I ever died and appeared before him."[10] During summers she attended Lutheran, Baptist, and Salvation Army churches, where she tried to understand the role God was playing in her life. She says she felt unsatisfied in prayer, questioned God's existence, and never enjoyed a stable relationship with God.

Eventually she took her questions about God's existence to a school matron. Instead of receiving appropriate answers to her doubts, young Betty was slapped, rebuked for disbelief, and commanded to get on her knees and pray for forgiveness. Of course, rather than feeling forgiven and restored, Eadie now felt "doomed to hell because of my lack of faith. . . . I was sure now that I could never be forgiven."[11]

Another time, she lay gazing at the stars one night and saw a moving ray of white light coming from a cloud. She screamed, terrified that this was Jesus' Second Coming, and that he would burn her for her sins.[12] Her father, whom she was with at the time, assured her that the spectacle was far less cosmic. It was only a search light. Though Eadie's early religious instruction was disappointing, she continued to "search for the true nature of God," even though she dreaded her "own death and the blackness that would follow."[13]

At age 15 she left school and joined her mother in Wyoming, where she married a neighborhood boy who later moved them to Reno, New Mexico. They divorced after having four children in six years. Betty married Joe Eadie in 1963. They had three sons, and five years after her last pregnancy she had a partial hysterectomy, which, she claims, resulted in her near-death experience (1973)—according to which God turned out to be far different from how the sisters at boarding school had described him.

HER STORY

Eadie's NDE, like many others, includes having an out-of-the-body experience (OBE), meeting angelic beings, feeling very peaceful, passing through a dark tunnel, encountering a being of light, having her life flash before her mind, and returning to her body with a sense of destiny. (I will discuss these and other features in more detail throughout the book.) The extraordinary difference between her story and most of the others is its depth of detail and extensive religious teaching. Herein lies the magnetism of *Embraced by the Light*.

As Eadie lay alone in the hospital room after her partial hysterectomy, she felt herself becoming weaker and weaker until she was paralyzed. A soft buzzing in her ears was followed by a strange surge of energy that drew her spirit upward through her chest and toward the ceiling. She looked down and beheld a lifeless body, which she realized was her own. Her disembodied spirit felt weightless, mobile, free from pain, and perfect.

She was joined by three "monks" dressed in light-brown robes and gold braided belts, who glowed from within. Eadie learned from them, through telepathic communication, that the four of them had been together for "eternities," meaning that she had known these men in a "pre-earth" world before she had been born. She took this to mean that "death was actually a 'rebirth' into a greater life of understanding and knowledge that stretched forward and backward through time."[14]

Despite the fascinating monkish companions, Eadie longed to see her family. Leaving her body behind, she somehow moved her "spirit body" from the hospital to her home "at tremendous speed." She saw her family, although they could not see her, and she received the impression that her children were spirits who had existed before their bodies were conceived. Convinced that her family could thrive even after her death, she instantaneously found herself back in the hospital with the three ethereal monks.

Almost immediately she heard a loud roaring sound, and was sucked through a long black tunnel at great speed. Other people, and even animals, were making the journey, although some appeared not to be moving ahead. Feeling completely tranquil and loved, she thought, "This must be where the valley of the shadow of death is."[15] But what happened next would make everything else pale by comparison. Jesus himself appeared.

After embracing her, Jesus said that her death was premature; it was not yet her time. Eadie then felt that there had been a purpose to her life. She did not want to leave Jesus because he loved her unconditionally, unlike the Jesus she had learned about as a child in boarding school. She says that all her questions were answered as Jesus' light permeated her with knowledge. In fact, she became "omniscient" during the experience, "able to comprehend the mysteries of the universe simply by reflecting on them."[16]

Eadie then visited large, archaic-looking looms that were used by spirit men and women to make clothing for those coming into the spirit world from earth. (The way this is done or its meaning is not explained.) She moved from the looms to "a library of the mind" where she again felt omniscient; she had but to reflect on a topic and all knowledge concerning that topic would become available to her. Further exploration took Eadie to a garden of unearthly colors, where a rose emitted music and she felt that she, God, and the rose were "all one." She also met other spiritual beings, including "Warring Angels," and saw far-flung "many worlds" created by God, as well as places where spirits prepare to take bodies.

Before returning to her body, Eadie experienced a life-review—something fairly common in NDEs. She reexperienced all the events of her life in a series of holographic images before a "council of men." She regretted parts of her life, but she wasn't judged by the men; rather, she judged herself with a new heavenly understanding. Jesus told her not to be too harsh with herself, and when the experience ended, he requested that she return to her body. After initially refusing, she relented. Following more heavenly fanfare, her spirit slipped back into her body.

After her descent back into the flesh, Eadie felt weighed down and chilled by her material body. She became depressed but was comforted by the angelic monks. These monks returned a few hours later to rescue her from an attack by hideous, hateful demons, whom the monks said were sent by the devil because he was upset at her decision to return to earth. So ends what has been called the most incredible NDE that has yet been claimed in modern times.[17]

WHAT EADIE LEARNED

While in her spirit body, Eadie was taught by Jesus, the monks, two spirit women, and others. She learned that all religions were necessary because of everyone's varying levels of spiritual understanding. Some religions may not have a full understanding of "the Lord's gospel," but they are still appropriate as stepping-stones toward an individual's "eternal progress."[18] In light of this, Eadie concludes that "we have no right to criticize any church or religion in any way."[19]

Eadie learned to her surprise "that Jesus was a separate being from God, with his own divine purpose." This went against her Christian upbringing, which had taught her "that God the Father and Jesus were one being."[20] She claims Jesus told her that all people were spirits in a pre-mortal world, and that they all had helped God create the universe and plan conditions on earth, including the laws of nature. These same spirits could later come to earth in bodies to further their spiritual growth. This would be their own choice; God would not intervene unless asked. So, she reasons, we are all volunteer earthlings, earth is not our natural home, and "sin is not our true nature"—although our spirits must constantly battle to overcome the flesh.[21]

Eadie also realized that love is supreme and that without love we are nothing. Any act of love is worthwhile, and we must love everyone in every way possible. Lack of love is what destroys, but God is unconditional love.

Next she was told that through the laws of the universe we can have access to incredible power. By going against these laws—by polluting, hating, being fearful, or overeating—we sin against the natural order and forfeit positive results. There is negative as well as positive energy. Positive thoughts attract positive energy and negative thoughts attract negative energy. Thus we create our environment through our thoughts, and "imagination is the key to reality."[22]

Eadie now understood how she could have had such negative feelings about Jesus as a stern judge to be feared; Jesus was always loving, but her negative thoughts had created negative feelings about him. "I understood again that fear is the opposite of love and is Satan's greatest tool."[23] With this new awareness, she was able to forgive her schoolteachers for giving her a false view of Jesus. She also "understood with pure knowledge that God wants us to become as he is, and . . . he has invested us with god-like qualities."[24]

She was taught that physical healing is available by having positive thoughts and drawing upon God's positive energy. Even illness and death have a natural place in the soul's progression and provide opportunities for growth. Sounding like New Ager Shirley MacLaine, Eadie says, "I saw that most of us had selected the illnesses we would suffer, and for some, the illness that would end our lives."[25] Everything has a purpose.

If we sin or break any laws, we need to forgive ourselves and move ahead in love, because "in the spirit world they don't see sin as we do here. *All* experience can be positive. All are learning experiences."[26] In other words, we don't have to ask God to forgive us; we only need to forgive ourselves. Sin is not the horrible thing that some religious people think God says it is.

Betty Eadie has come a long way from the fearful faith of her childhood. She no longer fears judgment and hell but believes she has been accepted by a loving Jesus and other marvelous spiritual beings. She does not worry about being rejected for her sins; she believes she has been accepted without question by God. Eadie's spectacular tour of other worlds has indeed transformed her view of God, human beings, death, and the afterlife. But are her new views genuinely biblical? Does she honor the Jesus to whom she dedicated her book?

2

HOW CHRISTIAN IS IT?

The one who first states a case seems right, until the other comes and cross-examines.

—Proverbs 18:17 NRSV

Having been raised in Christian settings, Eadie continues to identify herself as a Christian and to place a lot of emphasis on Jesus. For example:

> Of all knowledge . . . there is none more essential than knowing Jesus Christ. I was told that he is the door through which we will *all* return. He is the only door through which we can return. Whether we learn of Jesus here or while in the spirit, we must eventually accept him and surrender to his love.[1]

She also dedicated the book "To the Light, my Lord and Savior Jesus Christ." This dedication won her an interview on a Christian radio program in her hometown of Seattle, shortly after the book's release. Yet after the program aired, the interviewer wondered if Eadie's faith was truly biblical. He called me to discuss this and then invited me to be interviewed concerning Eadie's claims. I then read Eadie's book and realized that her testimony, for all its grandeur and wonderment, does not agree with biblical teaching at key points. Despite this, *Embraced by the Light* is often requested and sometimes sold at Christian bookstores.

As we look at points of disagreement between the teachings of Betty Eadie and those of the Bible, let us keep in mind that Eadie is not offering her opinions or commentary on the Bible or on any other religious book. Rather, she claims to have received a revelation directly from God concerning ultimate truths about God, life, and death. We should also remember the Bible's repeated warnings about false Christs (Matthew 24:5), false gospels (Galatians 1:6-10), false teachings (Acts 20:28-31), and its exhortation to "test the spirits to see whether they are from God" (1 John 4:1).

It is also important to understand that Betty Eadie is a Mormon, although this is veiled in the current edition of her book. *Embraced by the Light* was originally marketed in the heavily Mormon areas of Utah, Arizona, and Nevada as a Mormon testimony.[2] The first edition contained a one-page flyer entitled "Of Special Interest to Members of the Church of Latter-day Saints." It recounted Eadie's conversion to Mormonism and her desire to convert others.[3] The first edition also contained several obviously Mormon references that were altered in the mass-marketed version.[4] In order to reach a wider audience, Eadie's book was published by Gold Leaf Press, which was formed out of—and continues to be owned by—the Mormon publishing house, Aspen Books.[5]

As we test Eadie's testimony against Scripture, we should hold her accountable to her own words. When asked by a radio program host whether she was open to comparing her experience with the Bible, Eadie replied, "Oh definitely." The interviewer then asked, "Scripture remains authoritative?" To which Eadie responded, "It is authoritative."[6]

According to her account, Eadie does believe in a personal God who knows and loves her. She speaks of Jesus as God, Savior, and Lord. She mentions Satan and demons, as well as angels who guide and defend her. She rejects reincarnation[7] and briefly mentions the resurrection of the dead.[8] But this does not automatically make her teaching biblical. Despite her use of biblical words and Christian-sounding concepts, many of Eadie's statements contradict biblical teaching. It is quite possible for someone to use a biblical *vocabulary*, but not use the Bible as a *dictionary*.[9] With Eadie this is often the case. Her "Christian" vocabulary and ideas on spirituality are, as we will find, a strange mixture of mostly Mormon and New Age themes.

EADIE'S JESUS

Eadie was shown during her near-death experience that Jesus is a separate being from the Father. This belief squares with the Mormon doctrine that there is no Trinity but three separate gods.[10] However, it contradicts the affirmations of the Trinity in the Bible, which state that there is but one God (Deuteronomy 6:4) who exists as three distinct but coequal and coeternal divine persons: the Father (Matthew 6:9), the Son (John 1:1), and the Holy Spirit (Acts 5:3,4). Jesus said, "I and the Father are one" (John 10:30), a teaching that rules out a plurality of gods because of its emphasis on the oneness of essence shared by Jesus and the Father. Although Eadie at least twice speaks of "the Spirit of God,"[11] she fails to mention the Holy Spirit by name or as a distinct member of the Trinity. Yet the Bible claims he is as divine as the Father and the Son, and that his ministry is essential in enabling people to understand divine truths (John 14:26; Ephesians 3:5).

Eadie claims to have been embraced by the biblical Jesus, but her understanding of Jesus is unlike the Bible's view in many ways. She calls Jesus "Lord and Savior" but says absolutely nothing about his suffering and death on the cross, by which our salvation has been made possible. Yet the Jesus of the Gospels identifies this as the reason he came into the world. He needed to die and thereby to bear the penalty for sin on behalf of those enslaved by sin, in order that God's justice might be served and his love be demonstrated (John 3:16; Romans 5:1-8). The cross of Christ is at the heart of the gospel message, but it is conspicuously absent from *Embraced by the Light*.

The supreme authority, or lordship, of Jesus Christ is also missing from Eadie's account. When Jesus and "the council of men" asked Eadie to return to earth, she apparently suffered from no sense of obligation to obey Christ. Instead, she protested and bartered with them. She only consented after she was told about her "mission" on earth, and after she "*made them* promise that the moment my mission was complete they would take me back home.... They agreed to *my terms*."[12] In Eadie's view, Jesus is simply a member of a committee that suggests alternatives, but she herself has the final say about her life and death.

The Bible, however, says that Jesus, not any human, holds the keys (authority) of life and death (Revelation 1:18). And the apostle Paul, after speaking of Christ's incarnation and crucifixion, describes his exaltation:

> Therefore God exalted him to the highest place and gave him the name that is above every name, that at the name of Jesus every knee should bow, in heaven and on earth and under the earth, and every tongue confess that Jesus Christ is Lord, to the glory of God the Father (Philippians 2:9-11).

One who meets this Jesus is in no position to complain, barter, or demand. The tongue must confess his lordship and the knee must bow before his highness.

Eadie says that when she met Jesus she "knew that God was our mutual Father."[13] She seems to view Jesus more as an advanced spirit-brother than as absolute Savior and Lord. This, too, echoes the Mormon teaching that Jesus became divine through a spiritual process, just as we can.[14] But the Bible teaches that Jesus is the eternal Son by his divine nature (John 1:1). Those who have been forgiven of sin are made to be God's "sons" through adoption by God's grace (Ephesians 1:5; 1 John 3:1). Yet this adoption does not ever make us divine.

Eadie's heavenly visitation taught her that all religions should be accepted as appropriate for their adherents. This sentiment is a staple of New Age syncretism, which asserts that all religious roads eventually lead to God. But the Jesus of the Gospels is more concerned with whether or not someone has truly heard and obeyed His Word; for those who do not hear and obey will not be accepted. Jesus also declares that he is the *only* way to the Father (John 14:6; see also Acts 4:12). Likewise, the apostle Paul stated that even if an angel from heaven should declare a gospel different from the authentic one, he should be eternally condemned (Galatians 1:8,9). In the Bible, religious error is to be avoided at all costs (James 3:1,2; Titus 1:9). God's truth is nothing to take lightly.

PRE-MORTAL EXISTENCE

The pre-mortal, or preexistent, soul is taught repeatedly in *Embraced by the Light*. Eadie says that when she saw Jesus, she remembered him from a time before her physical birth. She also speaks of spirits awaiting and choosing their physical bodies. Here Eadie repeats Mormon teaching at one level and denies it at another. She agrees with Mormonism that people exist as spirits before birth, yet she contradicts Mormon teaching by claiming that each spirit chooses the body it will inhabit.[15]

The Bible teaches that a person comes into existence at the moment of physical conception and not before (Psalm 139:13-16; Zechariah 12:1). Though several biblical passages speak of

God "knowing" people before they were born (Isaiah 49:1; Jeremiah 1:5), this does not refer to their spiritual existence before physical bodies were taken. It simply means that God knows his plans for a person even before that person exists, similar to how an architect knows the building he has designed before the foundation has been laid.[16] According to the Bible, only Jesus Christ spiritually existed before his physical incarnation (John 1:1-3,14). According to Eadie, every human being existed before conception. This claim diminishes the biblical emphasis on the uniqueness of Jesus.[17]

The idea of the spiritual preexistence of the human soul is an ancient Greek and Gnostic belief that is also affirmed in Mormon[18] and New Age theology, but which does not square with the Bible. The notion that pre-mortal souls helped create the universe, as Eadie claims, diminishes the character of God as absolute Creator (see Genesis chapter 1).[19] God did not use any human assistance in fashioning the cosmos (John 1:3; Acts 17:25). In the book of Job, God states that Job was not there when God created the universe (Job 38:4; 40:1-5). By insisting on human cooperation with God in creation, Eadie breaks down the separation between the uncreated, all-powerful Creator and his finite creation.

In a television interview, Eadie used the idea of spiritual preexistence to explain the presence of evil in the world. She claimed that those who were tortured and killed during the Nazi Holocaust had chosen these horrific earthly situations before their birth.[20] She seemed to think this somehow made the situation more tolerable. But the ethical implications of such thinking are astounding.

Even if we grant Eadie's unbiblical ideas of preexistence, what sane spirit being would *choose* to suffer such unspeakable atrocities on earth? And if the Holocaust victims were not really victims at all but willing participants, then the Nazis should not have been morally condemned; they were simply enacting the wishes of their subjects. Surely, this is morally absurd.[21]

SIN AND SALVATION

Eadie's belief in the pre-mortal soul is tied in with her understanding of human nature and salvation. For her, the central human problem is a " 'veil' of forgetfulness" that results from taking on physical bodies.[22] We have a spiritual origin and identity, but embodiment causes us to be out of touch with this reality. Eadie echoes Plato's thinking when she comments that "birth is a sleep and a forgetting,"[23] which implies that the preexistent, disembodied state is far better than being in a physical body. Eadie's views are similar to the following lines from William Wordsworth, who was strongly influenced by Plato:

> Our birth is but a sleep and a forgetting:
> The Soul that rises with us, our life's Star
>   Hath had elsewhere its setting,
>   And cometh from afar:
>   Not in entire forgetfulness,
>   And not in utter nakedness,
> But trailing clouds of glory do we come
>   From God, who is our home.
> Heaven lies about us in our infancy!
> Shades of the prison-house begin to close
>   Upon the growing Boy,
> But he beholds the light, and whence it flows
>   He sees it in his joy.[24]

However, because Eadie claims we become embodied in order to grow spiritually, for her, embodiment is not as much of an imprisonment as Plato taught.

The biblical view is that in the final state after resurrection, believers will be in their perfected bodies (1 Corinthians 15:12-58), while those that reject God will suffer "everlasting contempt" (Daniel 12:2). The body, therefore, is not intrinsically inferior to the soul; it can be refashioned by the Creator so as to become eternal and perfect. Eadie mentions the resurrection of the dead in passing, but her basic ideas on the body and the soul are more Platonic, Gnostic, and Mormon than Christian.

Although Eadie uses the word *sin* several times (often putting it in quotation marks), she says that this "is not our true nature. Spiritually, we are at various degrees of light—which is knowledge—and because of our divine, spiritual nature we are filled with the desire to do good."[25] She does not regard sin as an offense against a holy God, but as a misuse of natural laws, due largely to ignorance. Repentance, therefore, involves forgiving oneself rather than confessing one's sin before God and asking for his forgiveness.[26] In fact, during Eadie's life-review, Jesus tells her to lighten up on herself and not to take her acts of wrongdoing so seriously.[27]

Eadie mentions nothing about repenting of sins committed *against God* (Psalm 51:4), or about placing trust in Jesus Christ in order to find forgiveness and eternal life (Matthew 11:28-30). She says we must "look within" and "trust our abilities,"[28] particularly the inherent power of our thoughts.[29] This emphasis on mind-power is like the New Age emphasis on the limitless power of human consciousness.

It follows from this that Eadie would tone down the biblical teaching about sin's entrance into the world. Eve "did not 'fall' to temptation as much as she made a conscious decision to bring about conditions necessary for her progression."[30] This is similar to Mormon[31] and Gnostic[32] teaching but alien to the Bible, which reveals that Eve, by disobeying God, succumbed to the serpent's temptation to sin, and that Adam fell into this sin along with his wife (Genesis 3; 2 Corinthians 11:3; 1 Timothy 2:14). The Scriptures teach that all people since the first couple have inherited a predisposition to sin (Psalm 51:5), which is so ingrained and severe (Mark 7:21-23; Romans 3:10-20) that it cannot be altered apart from God's supernatural help through the life, death, and resurrection of Jesus Christ (1 Corinthians 15:1-4; John 3:16). The apostle Paul put it clearly: "Believe in the Lord Jesus, and you will be saved" (Acts 16:31).

Eadie equates salvation with acquiring a kind of knowledge that leads a person from an earthbound perspective to a more spiritual one. Her words often affirm the Mormon doctrine of the eternal progression of the soul. She speaks of each individual's "eternal progress,"[33] and says that God is "the Man behind" the "Universal Power," and "that God wants us to become as he is, and that he has invested us with god-like qualities."[34]

Eadie seems to hold the Mormon belief that the heavenly Father is really a glorified man, and that, in time, we too can attain to this lofty status, as Jesus has. In other words, we are all potential gods. When Eadie claims she became omniscient during her near-death experience, she resonates with both the New Age idea that humans are inherently divine and the Mormon doctrine that humans can progress to deity.[35] Yet Paul clearly teaches that there is but one God and one mediator between God and finite, sinful humans—Jesus Christ (1 Timothy 2:5,6). While God is unlimited in his knowledge, humans will always be limited in what they know, both in this life and the next. Paul exclaims, "Oh, the depth of the riches of the wisdom and knowledge of God! How unsearchable his judgments, and his paths beyond tracing out" (Romans 11:33).

WORSHIP

The concept of worship, so central to the Bible's message, is entirely alien to Eadie's account. She never worships Jesus or the Father, nor do any of the other spiritual beings she encounters. Although the Bible does not record any near-death experiences (something we will take up in chapter 8), the first chapter of the book of Revelation tells of the apostle John's encounter with the resurrected and exalted Christ. John, a committed follower of Jesus Christ, beheld the glory of Christ face-to-face. But instead of being "embraced by the light," John fell on his face as a dead man. So overwhelming was the presence of Jesus that John prostrated himself in trembling worship. Afterward, Jesus comforted him, saying, "Do not be afraid. I am the First and the Last" (Revelation 1:17). In the biblical account, there is *first* awe and worship, and *then* comfort (see also Isaiah 6:1-8). In Eadie's account, there is only comfort.

When Eadie says she was "embraced by the light," so that she couldn't tell where her own light left off and the divine light began, it sounds like the New Age theme of merging and fusing with God. Eadie harmonizes with another New Age idea when she speaks of having always been a part of Jesus, which would mean she shared the same divine essence.[36] In a passage that might bring mystical chills to anyone enthralled with the New Age, Eadie says that during her near-death experience she gazed upon a rose, and "felt God in the plant, in me, his love pouring into us. We were all one."[37] If "all is one," there is no One to worship.

Yet the apostle Paul taught that although God is revealed through Jesus Christ, he "lives in unapproachable light" (1 Timothy 6:16). This clearly distinguishes the transcendent God from any of his creatures. The book of Revelation is filled with saints and angels worshiping before the throne of this transcendent God (Revelation 5). Eadie and her angels have other things on their minds.

DEMONS AND HELL

Embraced by the Light also omits any reference to hell. Eadie does refer to Satan and demons, but apparently they are unsuccessful in seducing anyone into hell. She teaches that all humans will return to their heavenly home through Jesus, thus excluding any divine punishment for the unrepentant. (It is unclear whether she thinks Satan and the demons will return to God.)

The Jesus of the New Testament, however, often preached on the awful state of those who reject the love of God. And he was not afraid to highlight the eternal torment of those whose actions betray their lack of trust in him (Matthew 25:46). In warning of spiritual imposters, Jesus declared:

> Not everyone who says to me, "Lord, Lord," will enter the kingdom of heaven, but only the one who does the will of my Father in heaven. On that day many will say to me, "Lord, Lord, did we not prophesy in your name, and cast out demons in your name, and do many deeds of power in your name?" Then I will declare to them, "I never knew you; go away from me, you evildoers" (Matthew 7:21-23 NRSV).

SPIRIT GUIDES

What are we to make of Eadie's "Warring Angels," or of the strange but lovable "monks" who assist her spiritual sojourn? She portrays them as benevolent spirit beings, but a biblically oriented approach cautions us to look beneath appearances. The Bible does speak of angels as God's messengers and instruments (Psalm 34:7; Hebrews 1:14). But according to many New Testament passages, clever impostors also populate the spiritual plane with intent to deceive the unwary. Satan himself can masquerade as an angel of light and his fallen angels as servants of righteousness (2 Corinthians 11:14). Assuming that Eadie had the NDE as she describes it (something we will discuss in chapter 7), her monastic escorts may well have been less than saintly, for the message Eadie received from them and the other spiritual beings is at odds with the Bible's teaching. Not everyone wearing a robe is reliable.[38] Fallen angels can lie; they can promise a false heaven.

HEAVEN

Eadie's heaven is a place of magnificent wonders and intense fulfillment. She rhapsodizes about the embrace of Jesus and the warmth of his unconditional love. For Eadie, heaven is our natural right; it is where we all will return; there is no threat of forfeiture. She even states that she knew she was "worthy" of Jesus' unconditionally loving embrace.[39] (She does not explain how one can be *worthy* of *unconditional* love.) These homecoming themes resonate within all of us because, as Solomon observed, God has put eternity in our hearts (Ecclesiastes 3:11), though we remain exiled far from the place for which we yearn.

If we turn to the Bible's explanation for our frustrated yearnings for eternity, we find that human rebellion against God's rule has severed our connection with the Creator. After our first parents' disobedience, God barred them and their descendants from eating of the tree of life, so that no one would be permitted to live forever in the state of sinfulness that henceforth would characterize humanity. Death came as a punishment for sin (Genesis 3:22-24; Romans 5:12-14).

Nevertheless, God provided a means of reconciliation for those who desire the everlasting life that they can never achieve on their own. Heaven is not a natural entitlement, not a human right, not a guarantee; for we are all unworthy of God. Heaven *is* the fulfillment of all that is good and true and beautiful, but it will be enjoyed only by those who humble themselves in repentance before God and accept his love as demonstrated through the sacrifice of Jesus, who is the "Lamb of God" and the focus of heaven's worship. C.S. Lewis put it well:

> In the end that Face which is the delight or the terror of the universe must be turned upon each of us, either with one expression or with the other, either conferring glory inexpressible or inflicting shame that can never be cured or disguised.[40]

Only for the adopted citizens of heaven, who have been redeemed through Jesus Christ's atonement, will the tree of life bloom again (Revelation 22:1-5).

ALLISON'S STORY

Unbiblical ideas about life and death may lead to tragic consequences. Allison ("Alli") Bierma was a popular, bright, active, and attractive 18-year-old high school senior from Greeley, Colorado, who was headed for college in the fall of 1994. Although Alli had been involved in a Christian church and had the support of a loving family, her life took a troubling turn. Her boyfriend went through a crisis of faith that was followed by depression and, tragically, his suicide.

Her family did not think Alli had been feeling suicidal or overly despondent. But on May 19, 1994, just a few days after her boyfriend's death, she disappeared. Her car was found in Rocky Mountain National Park, and a massive search began. After nearly three weeks, her body was found on June 5 at the bottom of a cliff. An eight-page, handwritten suicide note was in her pocket.

In the hope that her story might warn others, Alli's parents talked to me at length and let me read a copy of the note. As I read and reread Alli's note, I didn't detect the anger or deep despair often found in suicidal statements. She was clearly distressed over her boyfriend's death, but it seemed from the note that her decision to commit suicide was prompted more by anticipation of the afterlife than by disappointment with this life.

In the note, Alli underscored her love for her family and friends and urged them not to let her death bring them down. She told her family that "we must have planned to come to this world together and be a family a *long* time ago." She emphasized her longing to go "home" to be with "my Heavenly Father." Alli wrote that she could have learned more lessons on earth, but, "I will always continue to grow no matter where I am." She told her readers "to take some peace in knowing that I do not judge myself harshly," and to "take comfort in knowing that if God still wants me on this earth, I will not leave. . . . I will be more than willing to return if God asks me to." Alli asked her parents to "pray that I may have assistance on the other side." She said that "death is not so bad" and that on "the other side" she would be reunited with her boyfriend and eventually with everyone mentioned in the note. Near the end of the letter, Alli wrote, "Soon, we will all be together dancing and playing."

By now, Alli's comments should sound familiar. Her parents told me that Alli had read *Embraced by the Light* about six months prior to writing her suicide note, and that she had read it again shortly before she drove to the mountains, hiked to the top of a cliff, and plunged to her death. Her parents are convinced that some of the ideas expressed in the book played a key role in their daughter's death.

Certainly, a variety of factors apart from Eadie's book contributed to Alli's suicide—not the least of which was her boyfriend's suicide. Moreover, Betty Eadie never recommends or in any manner directly encourages suicide anywhere in *Embraced by the Light*. In fact, at one point Eadie even states that "we must never consider suicide" because this would deny us "opportunities for further development while here on earth."[41]

Nevertheless, the overall spirit and gist of Eadie's book does seem to glorify death and regard earthly life as something of a necessary evil. For example, at the end of her NDE, Eadie refused to leave the spirit world, crying out, "I'm *through* with earth!"[42] She did not agree to return until the men in charge[43] promised to bring her "back home" as soon as possible. She was "not willing to spend a minute on earth longer than was necessary."[44] And after Eadie had recovered from her surgery and had returned home, she "wanted terribly to return" to the "beauty and peace of the spirit world." It was with difficulty that she emerged from her depression and ceased "loathing" this life and "praying for death."[45] Moreover, Eadie's belief that we *choose* how we live and even how we die could also lead a person to conclude that her life is hers to give—or to take— however she pleases.[46] In view of these and other considerations, I believe Alli's parents may be correct in thinking that the unbiblical and overly romantic view of death and the after-life that is expressed in *Embraced by the Light* contributed to the fatal choice of an emotionally distressed young woman.

In a statement read at Alli's funeral, her father, who became a Christian through the ordeal, wrote:

> Alli fell victim to subtle distortions of the truth. She was searching for an end to the pain she was feeling inside. . . . She read books and developed concepts that glorified death and made her hunger "to go home." . . . However, the only way to get closer to God is through His Word, and that Word can only be found in the Bible.[47]

If Allison Bierma had been firmly grounded in the Word of God, she would have been less susceptible to being influenced

by appealing but false doctrine. If she had been thinking biblically, she would not have rationalized her suicide by believing
that she and her family had been together in heaven before
their earthly life, and that they would all be together in heaven
again (even though her father was not a Christian when she
wrote this in her note); that God would never reprove her no
matter what hurtful things she may do, so she need not judge
herself; that she would have the opportunity to choose to return
to earth if her death were premature; that death is a glorious
gateway to paradise for all those who pass through it; and that
heaven is a place where *everyone* eventually will be reunited in
eternal bliss.

The teaching in *Embraced by the Light* differs from biblical
teaching in several important respects. At many key points of
disagreement the biblical view is more likely than Eadie's to
restrain a person from suicide. Eadie's book teaches: 1) there is
no hell or punishment in the afterlife for anyone, 2) heaven is
everyone's eternal home no matter what, 3) death is not to be
feared by anyone for any reason, 4) God is not to be feared by
anyone for any reason, 5) we have no ultimate responsibility
before God for any wrongdoing, 6) we *choose* when and where
we come to earth, 7) the person who is near death *chooses*
whether or not to return to earth, 8) the purpose of life is the
spiritual development of the self, which continues for everyone
after death, 9) embodied, earthly life is a spiritual constraint,
from which we are released at death.

By contrast, the biblical view of life and death emphasizes:
1) our life on earth as a gift from God that we have no right
to resent, 2) our moral accountability to a holy God for the
obedient stewardship of our life, 3) hope of eternal life, which
comes only through trusting in the atoning work of Jesus Christ,
4) death as an enemy that will be finally defeated only at the
end of the age, 5) faith that any earthly situation can be redeemed by God for good, 6) the need to stay alive in order to

evangelize others so that they might inherit heaven and avoid hell.

It is not our right to choose when to be born or when to die, or how to proceed with our "eternal progress." But it is our responsibility to live in obedience to a sovereign, holy, and loving God.

A QUESTIONABLE LIGHT

Not only does Eadie's account diverge from biblical teaching in many ways, it also differs from what many other near-death experiencers have said about the life beyond, as we will see in upcoming chapters. It is significant that those who claim to give us experiential evidence for an afterlife often cannot agree on just what that life is or how we should prepare for it.

In order to make sense of these diverse claims, we need to understand the nature of the NDE and how to evaluate it. Eadie's story represents only one kind of NDE. Many others pose their own problems and contradictions. A number of significant questions remain to be asked. Did these near-death experiencers really die? Why are so many NDEs similar? Why do many differ? What are the spirit beings and the light that so many encounter? Is it possible to be deceived by this light? Should we believe what the near-death experiencer says about Jesus if it contradicts what Jesus said about himself? Do these experiences support any one religious view? Can these experiences be an initiation into the occult? How do they relate to Christianity—a movement whose followers claim was started by a man who rose from the dead? Why are so many people transformed after an NDE? Are NDEs igniting a higher form of consciousness or a higher stage of human evolution, as some New Age enthusiasts claim? We will explore these and other critical matters throughout the rest of the book.

THE BIBLE AND BETTY EADIE
ON SPIRITUAL TRUTH

The Bible	*Embraced by the Light*

GOD

One God, in three eternal persons (Deuteronomy 6:4; Matthew 28:18-20)	The Father is separate from Jesus (p. 47) A glorified Man (p. 61)

JESUS

God Incarnate (John 1:1-3,14)	A God (p. 44)
The Savior from sin through his cross (Romans 5:1-9)	Advanced spirit brother (p. 47)
Has authority over life and death (Revelation 1:18)	Does not have authority (pp. 118-19)
Worshiped in heaven (Revelation 5)	Not worshiped in heaven (pp. 40-53)

HOLY SPIRIT

Equally God with the Father and the Son (Acts 5:3,4)	Mentioned only as "the Spirit of God" (p. 110)
Holy (Ephesians 4:30)	Never regarded as holy
Illuminator of God's truth (Ephesians 3:5)	Not mentioned

HUMANS

Begin at conception (Psalm 139:13-16)	Exist as spirits before taking bodies (p. 31)
Did not help create the world (John 1:3; Job 38:4)	Helped create the world (p. 47)

Bible	*Embraced by the Light*

RELIGIONS

There is one true faith which Christ commissioned his disciples to preach to the world (Matthew 28:18-20)	All religions serve a good purpose (p. 45)
Jesus is the only way to God (John 14:6; Acts 4:12)	All religions are "stepping stones" to God (p. 45)
Non-Christian religions are not acceptable (Acts 17:29-31)	We should never judge a non-Christian religion (p. 46)

SIN

Eve sinned (1 Timothy 2:14)	Eve did not sin (p. 109)
We are sinful by nature (Romans 3)	Not sinful by nature, only ignorant (pp. 49-50)
We sin against a holy God (Psalm 51:4)	"Sin" is only breaking natural laws (pp. 54-61)

SALVATION

By faith alone through Christ alone (Ephesians 2:8,9)	By gaining knowledge; eternal progress (p. 45)
By trusting in Christ (Matthew 11:28-30)	By trusting ourselves; looking within (p. 94)

AFTERLIFE

Heaven or hell (Matthew 25:46)	All return to heaven through Jesus (p. 85)

Bible	*Embraced by the Light*

WORSHIP

Essential to our relationship to a holy God (John 4:23)	Not mentioned

BASIS FOR DISCERNING SPIRITS

Biblical truth, not feelings (1 John 4:1-4)	Feelings, not biblical truth (pp. 30-31, 41-42)

3

WHAT HAPPENS IN A NEAR-DEATH EXPERIENCE?

Dear God,
What is it like when a person dies? Nobody will tell
me. I just want to know, I don't want to do it.
Your friend,
Mike

—A child's letter to God

In the past 20 years, there has been an explosion of interest in NDEs. Scientists, theologians, philosophers, and other intrigued mortals have kept themselves busy trying to fathom the meaning of near-death experiences. But the NDE is not only a recent phenomenon. Medieval religion, for example, was very aware of people who said they had died and returned to life. Interestingly, these experiences were used to reinforce the religious ideals of the day. Several themes recur in medieval stories: the river of hell that terrorized the traveler, the flowery meadows of paradise beckoning, the throngs of heaven, the test-bridge on which one must travel without falling off into hell, and the externalization or recounting of deeds before God.[1]

During the modern period, otherworldly journeys continued to be reported and explored, but without meriting as much attention. Modern science and medicine tended to define reality narrowly by restricting it to the material realm. Consciousness was believed to end with the death of the body, and NDEs were discounted as hallucinations or even insanity.[2]

In our day, Raymond Moody overturned much of this skepticism. His rather modest first book triggered a revival of interest in the NDE.

RAYMOND MOODY: CREATING A PARADIGM

As a philosophy undergraduate, Raymond Moody was impressed by a lecture given by George Ritchie in 1965 concerning his postmortem experience, which later was published and became the bestseller *Return from Tomorrow* (1978).[3] After receiving a Ph.D. in philosophy, Moody began to collect stories of similar experiences. While in medical school he published *Life After Life* (1975), dedicated to Ritchie, as an informal account of 50 people he had interviewed in depth concerning a pattern of strange "death" experiences. The book featured a warm foreword by the pioneering student of death and dying, Elisabeth Kubler-Ross, author of *On Death and Dying*, who said that Moody's work "very much coincides with my own research."[4]

In the foreword to another Moody book, *The Light Beyond* (1988), noted sociologist and novelist Andrew Greeley proposed that Moody "has achieved a rare feat in the quest for human knowledge: he has created a paradigm."[5] Greeley was referring to Moody's earlier coining of the term "near-death experience" in his bestselling *Life After Life*. Moody coined the term to designate accounts of conscious experiences by people who were considered clinically dead by medical personnel or others. (We will discuss the concept of "clinical death" in more detail in chapter 7, but for now we can understand it to mean the cessation of vital biological functions.) Moody not only created a paradigm, or theoretical model, in his designation and description of the NDE, he also inspired a genre of writing that took the publishing world by storm.

Although *Life After Life* was advertised as establishing "proof" of an afterlife, Moody himself was much more cautious with his conclusions. He knew his research was strictly anecdotal and not scientific.[6] That is, his subjects were not part of a randomly selected sample, and he did not use the quantifiable methods of empirical science (although the book did inspire scientific studies). Rather than attempting to provide proof of the afterlife, Moody was content to correlate these unusual but recurring near-death experiences with the religious teachings about the afterlife found in the Bible, Plato, *The Tibetan Book of the Dead*, and the works of eighteenth-century mystic Emanuel Swedenborg. Nevertheless, Moody knew he was on to something significant. He concludes *Life After Life* insightfully:

> If the experiences of the type which I have discussed are real, they have very profound implications for what everyone of us is doing with his life. For, then it would be true that we cannot fully understand this life until we catch a glimpse of what lies beyond it.[7]

For all his tentativeness and apologies for not being scientific, Moody ignited a revolution in how people thought about life after death. The lid had been opened; the fascination with NDE testimonies would continue to grow.

What captivated so many readers were Moody's stories about people who, though clinically dead, did not lose consciousness but witnessed amazing things that seemed to conform to a basic pattern characterizing the NDE. From these stories, Moody identified 15 "common stages or events in the experience of dying."[8] These were not uniformly experienced by his subjects but were a composite of elements mentioned by those interviewed. He also emphasized that some people who had been clinically dead reported no experiences. And Moody's general picture included the experiences of people who came close to clinical death but did not actually die.[9] To highlight the similarities, we will compare Moody's common stages with Betty Eadie's account in *Embraced by the Light* (published 17 years after Moody's first book).

COMMON ELEMENTS IN
NEAR-DEATH EXPERIENCES

1. *Ineffability.* Near-death experiencers (NDErs) commonly report experiences in which time and space are so strangely changed that it is difficult to describe in words. Of course, this doesn't stop NDErs from trying to describe their experiences, yet they do so with some effort. Eadie herself sometimes strains to find the right words, but she doesn't hesitate to try to describe the majesty of her experience.

2. *Hearing the news.* Near-death experiencers usually report learning that they had died. They may hear a doctor or other medical personnel pronounce their death. One woman, whose heart stopped because of a drug allergy, heard the radiologist say to her doctor, "Dr. James, I've killed your patient."[10] Betty Eadie claims to have heard a nurse say, "We've lost her," when she was hospitalized at age four.[11] Yet she reports no such statement during her 1973 NDE; she claims no one was present at the time.

3. *Feelings of peace and quiet.* Many NDErs speak of having feelings of tranquillity and a sense of well-being at the initial stages of their otherwise disorienting experience. They often remark about the transition from being in pain and distress to feeling great peace. One man who "died" from wounds suffered in Vietnam said, "There was no pain, and I've never felt so relaxed. I was at ease and it was all good."[12] After her "death," Eadie speaks of feeling "no discomfort at all."[13]

4. *The noise.* People often report buzzing or ringing noises at the early stages of their NDEs, either pleasant or unpleasant. Eadie speaks of a "soft buzzing sound in [her] head"[14] and of "a deep rumbling, rushing sound."[15]

5. *The dark tunnel.* Many say they were pulled quickly through a long, dark space (tunnel, cave, funnel, valley) at the same time as they heard the noise.[16] Eadie's chapter "The Tunnel" describes this.[17]

6. *Out of the body.* One of the oddest and most remarkable aspects of many NDEs is the sensation of being lifted out of one's physical body so as to observe it from a distance, often with a feeling of calm detachment. Many observe what's going on in the hospital room or at the site where they had just "died." When they try to communicate with those left behind, they are not seen or heard. Eadie speaks of her spirit being drawn out through her chest, after which she observed that her body was "younger and prettier than I had remembered, and now it was dead."[18]

7. *Meeting others.* Spirits, angels, and deceased relatives or friends are often part of an NDE. Moody reports one woman who saw multitudes of deceased people hovering around the ceiling of a hospital room.[19] Other people report seeing assorted spirit beings who are not identifiable as ever having

been earthlings. Eadie recounts her monkish angels and various other spirit entities.

8. *The being of light.* One of the most controversial aspects of the NDE is the appearance of a luminous entity, which is often the most extraordinary and momentous element of the experience. This light usually is understood to be a person who radiates unconditional love and acceptance. Moody notes that though the description of the being is the same for all those who encounter it, the being is identified in different ways. Some say it is Jesus Christ; others an angel; others simply a being of light. This being communicates without words in a kind of mind-to-mind telepathic link. One woman said the being "asked if I was ready to die, or what I had done with my life that I wanted to show him."[20] According to Moody, the being never condemns and may even express some humor. This is certainly how Eadie explains being embraced by the light she calls Jesus.[21]

9. *The life-review.* The being of light often initiates a comprehensive replay of one's life, displayed in a panoramic or multidimensional manner (although this may occur without the being of light being present). As a result, individuals often better understand their past experiences and gain new insight into the consequences of their actions, both good and bad. One of Moody's cases said, "The best thing I can think of to compare it to is a series of pictures; like slides. It was just like someone was clicking off slides in front of me, very quickly."[22] Eadie calls it "holographic" because it is more than normal remembering; it is like a highly compressed and vivid reexperiencing of events.[23]

10. *The border or limit.* In a few instances, people report a place of demarcation, often viewed as a body of water, a gray mist, a fence, or a line. Moody speculates that each image may

express an underlying root experience, but he doesn't suggest what that might be. One woman saw a shoreline where deceased relatives were inviting her to join them. She refused.[24] Eadie does not relate anything like this.

11. *Coming back.* Moody says that the further one goes into an NDE, the less one desires to return to physical life. Some say they came back to help their families, some believe they were sent back by the being of light, and others say they were drawn back through the desires of loved ones. Some returned to their bodies without any explanation. Eadie argued strongly with Jesus and a "council of men" against her return; but after being shown her "mission," she acquiesced.[25]

12. *Telling others.* Most people are profoundly motivated to tell others about their experience, which they believe to be real and not imaginary. One person said, "It was nothing like an hallucination. I have had hallucinations once . . . and this experience was nothing like . . . them at all."[26] Moody also found that some persons were reticent to discuss their NDEs because they feared being misunderstood. In 1975 Moody wrote that he knew of no NDEr who had "gone out to preach about his experience on a full time basis."[27] This, of course, is no longer true. Today there is less skepticism regarding the NDE, due largely to bestsellers such as Eadie's book and Dannion Brinkley's *Saved by the Light* (1994). Although Eadie seems never to have doubted the spiritual reality of her NDE, she waited nearly 20 years to publish it.

13. *Transformations.* Moody notes that "there is remarkable agreement in the 'lessons,' as it were, which have been brought back from these close encounters with death."[28] The two most emphasized "lessons" are the need to cultivate love for others and the desire to grow in knowledge. Most NDErs' vision "left them with new goals, new moral principles, and a

renewed determination to try to live in accordance with them, but with no feelings of instantaneous salvation or of moral infallibility."[29] Moody also reported that in "a very small number of cases, persons have told me that after their experiences they seemed to acquire or to notice faculties of intuition bordering on the psychic."[30] (We will see in later chapters that other researchers believe that the incidence of psychic powers is significantly higher.) Eadie reports that her life was revolutionized by her NDE, that she was saved from religious confusion and the fear of God and death,[31] and that since then she has continued to have experiences with the spirit world.[32]

14. *New views of death.* Moody noticed that almost everyone he interviewed was no longer afraid of death. This doesn't mean that they now advocate suicide, or long for death, or do not fear the unpleasantness of a fatal illness. But they now believe they will survive their own death and that their afterlife will be blissful. One person commented, "I don't fear death. . . . I don't feel bad at funerals anymore. I kind of rejoice at them, because I know what the dead person has been through."[33]

Moody also noticed that no one painted a "mythological" picture of heaven and hell, and that the idea of a "reward-punishment model of the afterlife is abandoned and disavowed even by many who had been accustomed to thinking in those terms."[34] In Moody's cases, the being of light never condemned a person's sinful deeds, but responded with understanding and even humor. The idea of "cooperative development towards the ultimate end of self-realization" replaced the notion of "unilateral judgment" by God.[35] (Other NDE researchers, however, have found people reporting hell-like experiences; these will be considered in chapter 5.) The popular NDE picture of a nonjudgmental being who encourages "self realization" (God-consciousness) is very much what Eadie describes.[36]

15. *Corroboration.* Moody maintains that some out-of-the-body experiences that occur in NDEs can be corroborated. People claim to have watched the procedures performed on their dead bodies and later to have "amazed their doctors and others with reports of events they had witnessed while out of the body."[37] One girl claims to have gone out of her body from her hospital room and to have observed her sister in another room crying, "Oh Kathy, please don't die." She later baffled her sister by describing where she had been and the exact words of her lament.[38] Eadie says she observed her family during her NDE, but she doesn't mention any corroboration of this from them.[39]

In his next book, *Reflections on Life After Life* (1977), Moody drew on more NDEs and found four more rare but nevertheless recurring elements.

1. *The vision of knowledge.* Some NDErs spoke of experiencing a timeless realm, sometimes called a school or library, where all knowledge exists simultaneously. People reported being able to capture this knowledge and become temporarily all-knowing. A young woman told Moody, "Knowledge and information are readily available—all knowledge. . . . You absorb knowledge. . . . You all of a sudden know the answers."[40] Yet this knowledge and ability is lost upon returning to the body. Eadie's story echoes this experience.[41]

2. *Cities of light.* Several postmortem voyagers claim to have glimpsed cities of intense brightness and equanimity. This prompted Moody to revise his earlier comment that he had not heard of heavenly visions in the biblical sense. One woman described a city in which there were separate buildings, gleaming and bright. "People were happy in there. There were sparkling foundations . . . a city of light."[42] Eadie's elaborate rendition of heavenly landscapes makes Moody's look bland, although she doesn't speak of a city of light.[43]

3. *A realm of bewildered spirits.* Some NDErs report inhabitants of the other side who are *not* immersed in bliss; in fact, some seem downright confused. Moody thinks that these beings are unable to cut free of their terrestrial attachments or that their awareness is dulled in relation to other spirit beings, and that they must remain in this state until they can work through their inabilities to ascend. Others speak of these human spirits' frustrations at not being able to communicate with people on earth.[44] Eadie alludes to something like this when she describes those in the dark tunnel who are not moving ahead but are lingering or stuck.[45]

4. *Supernatural rescuers.* Some of Moody's examples include only brushes with death and not clinical death, so they don't qualify as NDEs. In this context, several individuals mentioned a supernatural being who saved them from impending death. But Moody does report one person who, given up as dead by doctors, was commanded to breathe by a voice taken to be God. Breathe this person did, and lived to tell about it.[46] Eadie doesn't speak of supernatural rescuers saving her from death, but she does mention angels who protected her from demons after her NDE.[47]

Despite the care with which he framed his reports and explanations, Moody, the philosopher, still had to admit that his work did not meet with the exacting standards of scientific investigation. But he did chart several ways in which other researchers could pursue the matter scientifically.[48] In the next chapter we move our discussion from the realm of anecdotes (stories that are not rigorously scrutinized) to more serious scientific studies of the NDE.

4

SCIENTIFIC INVESTIGATIONS

Death is never at a loss for occasions.

—Greek epigram

Raymond Moody's challenge to study the near-death experience more scientifically was taken up quickly by two serious researchers, psychologist Kenneth Ring and cardiologist Michael Sabom. Moody welcomed and recommended their work. In fact, "he told a Charlottesville conference on near-death studies in October 1982, 'If you want to read anything on the subject and haven't, I would not recommend my books now, but rather defer entirely to Kenneth's and Michael's books.'"[1]

KENNETH RING: NEW AGE RESEARCHER

Long before he encountered Moody's work, Kenneth Ring was strongly interested in "altered states of consciousness."[2] A professor of psychology at the University of Connecticut, Ring did a 13-month study of NDEs, which lifted him out of his depression, reoriented his professional activities, and produced "an extended spiritual awakening."[3] In the preface to his *Life at Death: A Scientific Investigation of the Near-Death Experience* (1980), Ring expressed the hope that his book would

---

produce a similar effect in his readers—a confession not often found in scientific studies.

Ring used scientific procedures to study a broad sampling of 102 survivors of cardiac arrest. He was interested in learning the nature of the near-death experience, the factors that might increase the likelihood of having one, and what its aftereffects might be. Of the 102 cardiac-arrest survivors, 48 had experienced an NDE. The 54 non-experiencers (those who had had cardiac arrests without NDEs) provided a control group, which had been lacking in Moody's investigations. Ring devised various measures for interviewing the 48 NDErs and for describing and recording their experiences. His formal findings tended to confirm Moody's informal work in many ways. But instead of coming up with 15 common elements of NDEs, Ring found five features that he called the "core experience." He writes:

> We now have sufficient scientific grounds for asserting that there is a consistent and remarkable experiential pattern that often unfolds when an individual is seemingly about to die. I will call this reliable near-death pattern the core experience.[4]

These core elements, in order of their occurrence, are feelings of peace, body separation (an out-of-the-body experience), entering the darkness, seeing the light, and entering the light. Usually, however, all five stages do not occur in one experience, and the earlier elements are more common than the later ones. For instance, only 10 percent of the NDErs entered the light, while 60 percent felt peaceful.[5]

Ring also described other NDE elements similar to Moody's, such as the life-review and the transformative effects of the NDE. Oddly, none of Ring's subjects spoke of a *being* of light, though some did refer to a "presence." For several reasons, however, Ring was not bothered by this apparent discrepancy between his research and Moody's accounts. First, the being of light had been reported by other NDE investigators besides Moody, which gave the phenomenon credibility outside of Ring's study. Second, although the being of light did not appear in Ring's study, the experience of light and a presence were documented. Third, the being of light is more likely to occur in cases of extended clinical death, which Ring's study didn't involve. Fourth, if experiencing the being of light is rare, it might be that Ring's study was too small to include instances of its occurrence.[6]

According to Ring's study, previous religious involvement did not significantly affect the likelihood of having an NDE. Those who clinically died without having an NDE did not change their religious ideas, but those who did have an NDE became much more spiritually sensitive afterward. This included "a sense of being closer to God, feeling more prayerful, taking less interest in formal religious services, but expressing greater tolerance for various forms of religious expression, and endorsing an attitude of religious universalism."[7] Ring referred to this as "spirituality" rather than "religion." Typically, the NDErs' fear of death was significantly reduced or eliminated, and their view of death became positive, often with an openness to reincarnation.[8] Ring thus found the NDE to be far more than a clinical issue. It changed people's lives.

In his next book, *Heading Toward Omega* (1984), Ring speculated that the NDE is an integral part of the change in consciousness that is contributing to a global evolutionary advance. He breathlessly ends the book:

> NDErs and others who have had similar awakenings may in some way prefigure our own planetary destiny, the next stage of human evolution, the

dazzling ascent toward Omega and the conscious
reunion with the Divine.[9]

Such speculation moves Ring beyond the experimental evidence.[10] It demonstrates a kind of millennial hope that is often associated not only with the study of NDEs but also with the worldview of New Age intellectuals such as Marilyn Ferguson, Jean Houston, David Spangler, Fritjof Capra, and Deepak Chopra.[11]

MICHAEL SABOM'S UNEXPECTED DISCOVERIES

Kenneth Ring's ground-breaking scientific study was followed by Michael Sabom's *Recollections at Death: A Medical Investigation* (1982). Unlike Ring, Sabom, a medical doctor, was quite skeptical of Moody's claims, but he was interested enough to study the subject scientifically. He and another researcher, Sarah Kreutziger, conducted a five-year study of patients who had been in a near-death condition, whether from cardiac arrest, coma, accident, or another cause. These patients were interviewed to see if they had undergone an NDE in their near-death states, and if so, what the experience was like.[12]

This research broadly supported Moody's conclusions. Sabom found the following elements to be characteristic of the NDE: ineffability, a sense of timelessness, a heightened perception of reality, a sense that one had died, enhanced emotions, and separation from the body.[13]

Sabom divided the experience into two parts: the autoscopic NDE and the transcendental NDE. The autoscopic aspect refers to viewing objects in the material world from a vantage point outside of one's own body. The experience begins with observing one's body and other people, hearing the goings-on, attempting communication with the living, and traveling by thought; it concludes with the return to the body and telling others about the NDE.[14] Sabom claimed that those who had the autoscopic experience were later able to relate information about their own condition as well as that of others—details that they could not possibly have known through their clinically dead bodies. This claim has proven controversial, but Sabom believes that these out-of-the-body observations of actual physical objects are verifiable.[15]

The transcendental aspect of the NDE involves passing through a dark region or void, seeing a brilliant source of light, describing scenes of a new environment, encountering others (whether Jesus, spirits, angels, or other beings), having a life-review, and then returning to one's body.[16]

Sabom found that most NDEs were either autoscopic or transcendental, but some had elements of both.[17] Both portions of the NDE occur out of one's body; but the autoscopic portion involves experiencing the physical world, while the transcendental portion takes place outside the physical environment of the departed body and involves interaction with elements of the spirit world.[18] As did Moody and Ring, Sabom concluded that there were significant variations among NDEs, but that the variations tended to occur within certain general patterns.

Sabom also found that neither a person's "age, sex, race, area of residence, size of home community, years of education, occupation, religious background, or frequency of church attendance" seemed to influence the likelihood of having an NDE.[19] Like Moody and Ring, he found that "almost every subject interviewed in this study indicated, in his own way, that his NDE had been a truly remarkable and important event in his life."[20] Some described the NDE as a " 'peak' event that had done more to shape the depth and direction of life goals and attitudes than any previous single experience."[21] Anxiety over death was drastically reduced, and the will to live was strengthened.

Contrary to Ring's findings, Sabom saw no change in the basic religious beliefs of NDErs. Rather than being changed, the religious views of NDErs were "commonly strengthened by the experience itself," and this was manifested in "a marked increase in formal religious activity and commitment."[22] This finding deviates markedly from Ring's observation that NDErs tended to move away from traditional religion and toward a more private and New Age spirituality.

The following dialogue illustrates the increase in traditional religious belief and practice that occurred as a result of one man's NDE:

Sabom: What do you think this episode [the NDE] was?

Patient: I couldn't really say, but I think that's when Christ came into my life. . . . It completely changed everything as far as my way of living. Before that I drank beer and whiskey and a lot of things I wouldn't do now. . . . I couldn't wait until I got out of the hospital [after the NDE] to go to church. The pastor said he had never seen anyone so anxious to come forward and accept Christ as I was.

Sabom: Before your experience, did you attend church?

Patient: No. I never went to church.[23]

The patient went on to say that he was now serving "the good Lord" by working with the Veterans Volunteer Service, helping people in the hospital and playing tapes of his church's services for them.[24]

MORSE'S CHILDREN OF THE LIGHT

While Moody's books were popular but not scientific, Ring's and Sabom's were more scientific but not as popular. Another writer, Seattle pediatrician Melvin Morse (who wrote the introduction to *Embraced by the Light*), combined the popular with the scientific in two bestselling books, *Closer to the Light* (1990) and *Transformed by the Light* (1992).

Morse's fascination with the subject began with one of his young patients, Katie, who had been found floating facedown in a swimming pool. Although her chance of survival was only around ten percent, Morse was able to resuscitate her and she completely recovered, despite massive brain swelling and the need to have an artificial lung. When the shy nine-year-old recounted what had happened while she was being resuscitated, Morse was stunned. Katie said she had been escorted through a tunnel with Elizabeth, whom she identified as a guardian angel. She met her deceased grandfather and two souls waiting to be born (a similarity to Betty Eadie's account). She saw things that were happening at home, which her parents later verified. Then she saw "the Heavenly Father and Jesus." When Jesus asked if she wanted to see her mother again, she said "yes" and found herself back in her body.[25]

Morse began research on the NDEs of children in order to find answers to several questions. Does one need to be near death to have an NDE? Is there an area of the brain that is responsible for NDEs? Are there any aspects of NDEs that previous research had missed? How do NDEs affect adults who had had them as children?

To answer these questions, Morse initiated the "Seattle Study," which involved a research team of eight people who were experts in various aspects of the NDE. Morse selected a control group of 121 children who had life-threatening conditions but were not near death.[26] For the study group he chose

12 children who had clinically died and would have remained dead without resuscitation procedures. Both groups were interviewed about their religious beliefs and their experiences of being near death or of having a life-threatening sickness.

The Seattle Study concluded that one must be near death to have an NDE, for only those in the study group (and no one in the control group) had ever experienced anything resembling an NDE.[27] Also, the young NDErs reported the same kinds of core experiences that Moody, Ring, and Sabom had discovered, but with some differences. Children were much less likely to experience life-reviews, presumably because their lives till then had been short; and they were more likely than adults to decide for themselves to return to their bodies.[28]

Morse makes much of the experience of light, which he says occurs in "nearly every near-death experience of children."[29] This experience, Morse thinks, may represent a "rebirth" after death.[30] The children speak of a brilliant light that radiates love, forgiveness, and energy. Some descriptions are of a personal being; others speak more of an energy or power. Morse cited a report from another study in which a 14-year-old boy described the light as "all being, all beauty, all meaning for all existence. It was all the energy of the Universe forever in one place."[31] Morse also maintained that some children have psychic experiences during their NDEs. He cited a report by one woman, who claims to have seen her future husband and two children during an NDE when she was a teenager.[32]

Morse suggested that NDEs can be partially explained by the activity of an area of the brain which he calls the "seat of the soul."[33] But he admitted that the phenomenon of light cannot be explained purely by physical causes.[34] At any rate, he concluded (as did Moody, Ring, and Sabom) that the NDE has a transformative effect on those who experience it. And, like Ring, Morse wrote a second book, *Transformed by the Light*, in order to explore the aftereffects of the NDE.

Morse created the "Transformations Study" in order to answer the question: "Are there transformative effects from the near-death experience that can be documented?"[35] He selected 350 subjects, 100 of whom had reported NDEs. The other 250 formed five different control groups. From his survey questions, Morse found that NDErs have less anxiety concerning death and a greater zeal for living compared with those who had not had NDEs. Typical NDEr responses about death included: "It's not death, it's another kind of life," and "Death? Not worried about it at all."[36]

Near-death experiencers also showed a greater concern with expressing love and gaining knowledge, and they were better able to talk about their purposes for living. For example, Spencer Christian, weatherman on the "Good Morning America" television program, claims to have had a childhood NDE that left him with the strong feeling that "it is the purpose of my life to pass on as much positiveness as I can every day of my life with every person I meet."[37]

Morse claimed that as a result of their experiences NDErs showed signs of enhanced intellectual ability and expanded psychic ability. After studying NDEs for more than a decade, Morse concluded that virtually *all* the people who have had the experience—whether homemakers, lawyers, secretaries, journalists, musicians, or doctors—"report psychic experiences as a result of the NDE."[38] When asked, NDErs tend to believe they have greater abilities to predict the future. One woman, who had had an NDE after a suicide attempt at age 12, says, "On a regular basis, I dream what will happen the next day." She dreams about conversations before they happen, and she dreamed about the sudden death of her uncle due to a heart attack. Although he had been in perfect health, he died just as she had dreamed.[39] The NDErs that Morse tested had had "more than four times the number of validated psychic experiences as the normal and seriously ill [control] group" and "twice the number of verifiable psychic experiences as those we tested who claim to be psychic."[40]

Morse believes that the NDE offers hope to us all. Concluding *Transformed by the Light*, he writes:

> The knowledge that these visionary experiences at the point of death are real and transformative validates us as spiritual beings. These experiences teach us many things, but most important they show us that there is a foundation of life from which all of us spring. . . .
>
> Human beings have the ability to be inspired by a light which has the power to transform them. We do not have to die to learn from this experience. We only have to be open to its message.[41]

THE OUT-OF-THE-BODY EXPERIENCE

Not all scientific investigators share Ring's and Morse's enthusiasm about the reality and spiritual benefits of the NDE. A variety of scientific criticisms have attempted to show that it is not a genuine spiritual experience. Critics argue that the different aspects of the NDE—feelings of peace, leaving the body, the dark tunnel, the appearance of spirit beings, the being of light, and so forth—can be explained solely on the basis of neurochemical events in the brain. NDEs are simply hallucinations or misperceptions caused by the dying brain or by the effects of medication given to those in emergency situations. For such critics, there is no reason to believe that NDErs experience anything outside of their physical bodies. If this is true, then the NDE tells us nothing about spiritual reality or the afterlife.

Many of these criticisms are dealt with in the Appendix, "Is It All in the Brain?"—which concludes that there is strong evidence that some NDEs have a spiritual component (which can include spiritual deception).[42] But before finishing our overview of scientific research into the NDE, we should look at the one aspect that is most resistant to being explained away in terms of neurological function—namely, the viewing of one's physical environment from outside of one's body. This is generally referred to as the out-of-the-body experience (OBE).

Susan Blackmore, a skeptical psychologist, believes that the physical universe is all that exists, and that consciousness is limited to and dependent upon the physical brain; there is no immaterial soul that can be distinguished or separated from the body.[43] Therefore, she attempts to explain the OBE as nothing more than a sophisticated deception produced by the brain.

Blackmore herself experienced a full-blown OBE that did not involve an NDE but was induced by using hashish. After hovering near the ceiling, she moved through the roof and "clearly observed the red of the roofs and the row of chimneys" before she flew "on to more distant places. . . . I visited Paris and New York and flew over South America."[44] Blackmore later discovered that the roofs she thought she saw were actually gray and not red and that the chimneys were not there at all.[45] This refuted the reality of her OBE. Blackmore's OBE also included having a "duplicate body" that left her physical body; this is unlike the vast majority of OBEs that occur during an NDE.[46]

Blackmore does not dismiss the OBE element of the NDE simply because something like it can occur during drug experiences. In fact, OBEs occur in a variety of settings and are experienced by 15 to 20 percent of the general population.[47] Blackmore argues that sensory deprivation and a distorted body image (confusion as to the parameters of one's body) are important factors in causing OBEs. Because both of these factors are present in many NDEs, they explain the occurrence of an OBE without recourse to the idea that the soul has left the body.[48]

Blackmore also claims that reports about actual events perceived during an OBE can be accounted for on the basis of a patient's residual consciousness even while under an anesthetic (which has been documented) or in other "unconscious" states. In other words, the OBE is constructed out of one's imagination, one's residual awareness while anesthetized or unconscious, and educated or lucky guesses as to what might have been happening while one was clinically dead.[49] But can these natural factors adequately account for all OBEs?

Sabom's work on the OBE element of the NDE was groundbreaking and remains controversial. He studied 32 NDEs in which NDErs observed their bodies from the outside (what Sabom called "autoscopic descriptions").[50] Of these, 26 accounts involved only general descriptions of the scene of the clinically dead body. The lack of detailed description of the physical environment in these cases is explained, according to Sabom, by the NDErs' preoccupation with the "unique and pleasant qualities of the experience" and their "overall amazement at what was occurring."[51] However, six of the NDErs did give detailed accounts, and Sabom found these cases to be unexplainable on the basis of natural phenomena.

In one case, a middle-aged security guard from north Florida had suffered a massive heart attack and cardiac arrest. Afterward, the man described the following emergency procedures which had been administered to his clinically dead body:

> His body being lifted off the floor onto a stretcher; his legs being strapped to the stretcher; a sharp blow to his chest by a "doctor," followed by manual chest compression; his body being wheeled down the ER hall on the stretcher to meet the emergency cart with

the defibrillator [shock device to restart the heart], cardiac monitor and other resuscitative equipment; the insertion of a plastic airway into his mouth; the cardiac monitor; the injection of medications into his heart; two attempts at cardiac defibrillation and the regaining of physical consciousness.[52]

This man's description not only agreed with his medical records (which had not been made available to him), but portrayed the proper sequence of CPR technique. After getting to know the man, Sabom judged that he had no more than a "layman's knowledge of medicine," and that it was "evident that many of the details he recalled were given in response to my own probings and were not volunteered, as might have been expected from an informed individual attempting to 'reconstruct' the events of the resuscitation from a detailed knowledge of the procedure."[53]

Sabom was particularly struck by the fact that when he referred to the electric defibrillation instruments by using the word *paddles* (their common medical term), the man objected. "They weren't paddles, Doctor. They were round disks with a handle on them. No paddles."[54] His description was quite accurate but showed his ignorance of medical jargon.

In another case, a retired Air Force pilot had undergone an NDE during a massive heart attack and cardiac arrest. Afterward, he too described the activities of the medical personnel: an injection, the cardiac board placed behind his back, the movement of the defibrillator dials, the use of the paddles, the resulting jolt to his body from three separate shocks, the external cardiac massage, and the use of a pale-green oxygen mask.

Although detailed medical records were not available, his description also corresponded to the procedures that normally would have been used in such a case—procedures the man said he was ignorant of before the NDE. Sabom was especially impressed by the man's detailed description of the defibrillator needles which perfectly matched the kind of machine used at the time. The man also used technical medical terms such as "lidocaine pushes," "defibrillator," and "watts-seconds," which he says he learned while being out of the body and paying close attention to the situation. Sabom was convinced that the man "would have no reason to lie about these statements."[55]

In the four other detailed accounts Sabom also found descriptions that matched the medical situations. None of the patients appeared to have had prior knowledge of the medical procedures that were performed. In one of these cases, a 60-year-old retired laborer described the goings-on outside the scene of his resuscitation. He told of seeing his wife, oldest son, and oldest daughter standing in the hospital hall at the time of his cardiac arrest. His family members later confirmed the accuracy of his description, and said that he could not physically have seen them down the hall from where he lay unconscious.[56]

Betty Eadie also claims to have seen her family in their home while her body lay in the hospital bed.[57] But in typical Eadie fashion, she gives no corroboration.

In assessing his cases, Sabom concluded that the reports "appear to be fairly specific for the actual resuscitation being described and are not interchangeable with the clinical circumstances of other near-death crisis events."[58] Therefore, these OBE reports could not be explained by saying that the patients' prior knowledge of medical practice was generalized to fit the specific situation.[59]

Blackmore believes that details of emergency situations could be gained after the event and then read back into it. But Sabom argues that the specific information which patients relate after their OBEs would not "likely be explained to a patient recovering from a cardiac arrest."[60] Moreover, one of the patients Sabom interviewed said that when the attending doctor

> told me I had a close call and died . . . I told him, "Dr. B, I couldn't have died. I knew everything that went on." I told him when he came up under my right armpit and changed his mind and went to the other side. He said it was impossible and that I couldn't have possibly seen that, and that I was legally dead at that time. He just shook his head. . . . And I asked, "Am I right?" He said, "Yes, you're right!"[61]

Clearly, this man was not retelling what he had already been told about his medical crisis. All he knew was what he had seen during his OBE.

Sabom was also impressed by the fact that this patient observed an extraction of blood during his OBE and later described it as an injection, for that is how it would have appeared when viewed from above by an untrained observer.[62] Blackmore responded skeptically to this, pointing out that patients sometimes can hear and feel what is happening while they are "unconscious." This particular patient probably felt the jab into his body and then remembered it later as a shot.[63] However, it seems unlikely that the man would have felt the needle because he claimed that during his OBE he "had no feeling"[64] and "felt no pain whatsoever."[65] Furthermore, NDErs always report losing all sensory contact with their body during the OBE and often speak of being jolted by pain upon returning to their bodies.[66]

Even if some "unconscious" patients are somewhat conscious of their medical treatment, it is improbable that this would have been the case with all 26 subjects cited by Sabom—especially considering the detailed accuracy of six of the reports.

Finally, the natural mechanisms that Blackmore uses to explain away OBEs cannot possibly apply to cases in which NDErs observed events at a considerable distance from their clinically dead bodies and which were afterward confirmed by others. The only naturalistic response to these kinds of OBE cases is simply to deny all such stories as fabrications or misinterpretations.

Documentation of corroborated OBE "sightings" has been infrequent in scholarly literature (although anecdotal reports of such things abound). However, a recent article in the *Journal of Near-Death Studies* gives three examples of verified perception during the NDE. In one of these, a woman traveled up to the hospital roof during her NDE and saw a red shoe. She later told this to a "skeptical resident," and he fetched a janitor who found the predicted shoe.[67]

It seems, then, that a merely physical explanation of the OBE aspect of the NDE cannot account for the kinds of remarkable evidence found in many reports. Science, therefore, has not disproved the claim that the soul leaves the body during the NDE.[68]

MORE QUESTIONS TO BE ANSWERED

If at least some NDEs are spiritually "real," what kind of spiritual reality is encountered during the experience? What exactly is the message of the NDE? Should we be "open to it" as a stimulus to better living and better dying? Is there more to an NDE than meets the senses? As the study of NDEs has moved beyond the anecdotal to include the scientific, a general pattern has emerged. Many (but not all) people who clinically die continue to be conscious and to perceive things in both the physical and spiritual realm. Moreover, Moody, Ring, Sabom, and Morse report that in almost every case the NDE is an overwhelmingly positive experience.[69]

However, the positive NDE appears to be mostly a modern occurrence. The popular NDEs that we hear about today are quite unlike the near-death accounts that preceded our time. Modern NDEs dispense with

> the bad deaths, harsh judgment scenes, purgatorial torments, and infernal terrors of medieval visions; by comparison, the modern other world is a congenial place, a democracy, a school for continuing education, and a garden of unearthly delights.[70]

Nonetheless, not a few modern NDErs *have* recounted bone-chilling and even hell-like experiences after clinical death. As we will see in the next chapter, one man frantically begged his resuscitating doctor not to lose him because, as he exclaimed, "I am in hell!" These unsettling accounts, as well as their spiritual implications, must be fairly and seriously considered if the entire meaning of the NDE is to be understood. We will investigate the dark and frightening NDEs in the next chapter.

NEAR-HELL EXPERIENCES

Do not be afraid of those who kill the body but cannot kill the soul. Rather, be afraid of the One who can destroy both soul and body in hell.

—Jesus Christ (Matthew 10:28)

In the first four chapters, we surveyed anecdotal reports and scientific research on the NDE, and discovered that it is no oddity. Near-death experiences have been testified to, systematically studied by competent authorities, and certainly seem intensely real to whomever has one. But are these experiences reliable guides to the reality of the afterlife? Do they disclose that death is nothing to fear, that everyone is guaranteed an eternity of sublime peace and bliss? If so, then why do these seeming realities often disagree with each other? Even in NDEs that are blissful, the nature of the bliss and the identity of the being of light often are reported differently. And, contrary to what many evangelists of the afterlife would have us believe, not all NDEs are blissful. Researchers of the NDE have encountered a variety of unpleasant near-death experiences; some even sound a lot like hell.

PARADISE LOST

Maurice Rawlings is a cardiologist who has resuscitated

dozens of patients. The experience of resuscitating one patient in particular inspired him to write *Beyond Death's Door* (1978). While he was testing a man for a heart problem on a treadmill machine, the man went into cardiac arrest and began to turn blue. Rawlings immediately began external heart massage while a nurse administered mouth-to-mouth resuscitation. Other nurses brought in a breathing mask and pacemaker equipment.

The patient would occasionally regain consciousness but then lose it again whenever Rawlings would interrupt the compression of his chest in order to perform other life-saving procedures. Each time the man revived, he would scream, "I am in hell!" He would plead with Rawlings not to let him slip back into death, and would cry out repeatedly, "Don't stop!" This was unusual because CPR is a violent and painful procedure and many patients complain about the pain when they regain consciousness.

As Rawlings continued CPR, the man became increasingly alarmed and terrified. His pupils were dilating, and he was perspiring and trembling. Again he pleaded, "Don't you understand? I am in hell. Each time you quit [the CPR] I go back to hell! Don't let me go back to hell!"[1] Rawlings wrote that "after three or four episodes of complete unconsciousness and clinical death from cessation of both heartbeat and breathing,"[2] the patient cried in desperation, "How do I stay out of hell?"[3] Rawlings told the man what he remembered from Sunday school, and the man asked Rawlings to pray for him. Unusual as the context was, and although Rawlings was not a committed Christian at the time, he led the man in this prayer:

> Lord Jesus, I ask you to keep me out of hell.
> Forgive my sins.
> I turn my life over to you.
> If I die, I want to go to heaven.
> If I live, I'll be "on the hook" forever.[4]

The man's condition stabilized, and he was taken to a hospital. A few days later, Rawlings questioned this man about his hell-like experience and found that he had forgotten it! Rawlings thinks that the experience had been so unnerving that it was repressed. Even so, the man became a committed Christian and a regular churchgoer after his experience of hell.[5]

Because he lost the memory of his NDE, we know little of what Rawlings's patient experienced beyond his feelings of torment and his repeated pleas to be kept out of hell. We know that he clinically died several times, and we know what he claimed to be experiencing. We can infer that, unlike the reports so commonly publicized, there was no feeling of peace, no welcoming being of light, and no dissipating of the fear of death. Instead, the fear of death and hell intensified to the point of frenzy and desperation.

In *Beyond Death's Door* and in the sequel, *To Hell and Back* (1992), Rawlings discusses other cases of hell-like NDEs. These reports offset the almost uniformly positive accounts of NDEs given by Eadie, Brinkley, Moody, Ring, Sabom, and Morse.

Moody originally claimed in *Life After Life* that he had "not heard a single reference to a heaven or a hell anything like the customary picture to which we are exposed in this society."[6] He modified this in *Reflections on Life After Life* by stating that he had heard of several heavenly NDE scenes[7] and of cases where "beings were 'trapped' in an apparently most unfortunate state of existence."[8] George Ritchie, whose NDE originally inspired Moody's research, spoke of seeing pathetic souls in the afterlife who were in bondage to the effects of such vices as suicide, hatred, and self-absorption.[9] These vices, said Ritchie, had blinded them from the light of Jesus.[10]

P.M.H. Atwater, who is both an NDEr and an NDE researcher, describes several negative experiences in her books *Coming*

Back to Life: The After-Effects of the Near-Death Experience (1988) and *Beyond the Light: What Isn't Being Said About Near-Death Experience* (1994). In the late 1960s she visited a woman at St. Alphonsus Hospital in Boise, Idaho. The woman, who had suffered a heart attack, was "chalk-white with fear" when Atwater arrived. She reported that while clinically dead she had floated above her body, entered a dark tunnel, and headed toward a bright light. So far so good. But when she reached the light, she found a barren landscape crammed with nude, zombielike people standing elbow to elbow who did nothing but stare at her. She started screaming, which snapped her back into her body. But she did not stop screaming until she was sedated. Despite the many churches that tell people about hell and how to avoid it, the woman "declared death a nightmare, then cursed every church throughout all history for misleading people with rubbish about any kind of heaven. She was inconsolable."[11]

Atwater also conversed with an elderly man and woman at the same hospital who had been equally frightened through similar NDEs after experiencing heart failure. Another man at that hospital, whom Atwater was not allowed to visit, was reported to have been muttering about "hills and hills of nude people staring."[12] Although Atwater holds to a New Age perspective, which leaves no room for belief in hell, she concluded that "these people were absolutely convinced there is a hell."[13]

Atwater later observed that although "most researchers of the near-death experience (NDE) report that unpleasant cases are quite rare, numbering less than one percent of the thousands thus far investigated," she had found an "abundance of [negative] cases: 105 out of the more than 700 I have queried."[14] And she is not the only person to have noticed this. When a surgical nurse at a hospital in Phoenix, Arizona, met Atwater, she said to her,

> I know who you are; you're the woman I just saw
> on television. You're the gutsy one who talks about
> negative near-death experiences. Keep doing it. Don't
> stop. . . . We have lots of near-death cases . . . and
> almost all of them are the negative kind. You know
> what I mean—people wind up in hell.[15]

At a 1990 conference on near-death studies, respected NDE researcher Bruce Greyson commented that negative NDEs had gone largely unreported and unstudied because "people like himself had not been asking the right questions to identify those who might have undergone 'dark' or distressing episodes."[16] He candidly confessed, "We didn't try to find them because we didn't want to know."[17] Greyson has since published an article about negative NDEs,[18] and he also has advertised for reports "from anyone who has had an unpleasant NDE of any type, including . . . experiences that are frightening; experiences of an eternal void or nothingness; and hellish or demonic experiences."[19]

Atwater's research has pointed her toward "universal elements" common to both heaven-like and hell-like NDEs. These elements tend to occur in "the same basic sequence pattern": an out-of-body experience; moving through a dark tunnel or some kind of darkness; seeing a light ahead; entering into that light; then quickly entering another realm usually filled with people, landscapes, and sometimes animals.[20] Although there is some structural similarity between heaven-like and hell-like NDEs, there is also a clear difference. Atwater summarizes:

Heaven-like Cases	**Hell-like Experiences**
friendly beings	lifeless or threatening apparitions
beautiful, lovely environments	barren or ugly expanses

Heaven-like Cases	Hell-like Experiences
conversations and dialogue	threats, screams, silence
total acceptance and an over-whelming sensation of love	danger and the possibility of violence, torture
a feeling of warmth and a sense of heaven	a feeling of cold (or temperature extremes) and a sense of hell[21]

Hell-like NDEs always seem to involve an attack of some kind or a painful shunning or taunting. Themes of good and evil and beings like angels and devils are also commonplace. The devil may even appear in an effort to win the battle for the NDEr's soul.[22]

Atwater does not interpret these experiences as evidence for the biblical understanding of heaven, hell, angels, demons, and the devil. She views them as purgatorial and pedagogical, in that they serve as an internal cleansing and as a means of learning more about spirituality.[23] Nevertheless, her work challenges much of the current thinking on the NDE by chronicling, evaluating, and publishing these hell-like experiences.

Another NDE researcher, Charles A. Garfield, worked with 215 patients who were dying of cancer. Of the 22 percent who told him about their NDEs, four groups formed. The first group reported positive states, such as Moody described. The second "experienced demonic figures, nightmarish images of great lucidity."[24] Group three told of dreamlike images, which were sometimes blissful, sometimes terrifying, and sometimes a mixture of both. The last group described a void or tunnel, or both, in which they were drifting. Garfield observed, "Almost as many of the dying patients I interviewed reported negative visions (encounters with demonic figures, and so forth) as reported blissful experiences, while some reported both."[25]

Clearly, the presence of something like hell in a number

of NDEs questions the popular belief that the afterlife experienced by the clinically dead is always positive, uniformly blissful, and unconditionally accepting of everyone. The truth is that testimonies from NDErs are mixed on whether the afterlife will be pleasant or unpleasant.

This is not the only reason NDEs are unreliable guides to the afterlife. The fact is, the NDE is not about the ultimate or final state of the soul, because near-death experiencers return only from *clinical* death.[26] One day they will die again for the last time and will not return to report their findings. We must at least allow for the *possibility* that their final state may be quite different from the conditions they reported in their NDEs. What the NDE does indicate is that the soul can exist apart from the body and experience a spiritual dimension that is not normally perceived during physical life on earth.[27]

IS IT SAFE TO DIE?

How, then, do we account for the negative NDEs? How should we understand them? Is it always safe for everyone and anyone to die?

The original research of Maurice Rawlings was criticized by Kenneth Ring and others for not being scientific enough. Rawlings did not carefully detail how many people he had interviewed personally versus the number of secondhand reports he had received. Nor did he specify the amount of time that had elapsed between the NDEs and the interviews. Ring also questioned Rawlings's theory that repression may occur if one doesn't interview a negative NDEr quickly after clinical death, and that negative NDEs, therefore, may occur more frequently than reports indicate. Ring pointed out that this theory is based only on one verifiable case, and that other medical personnel have resuscitated patients and have interacted with them immediately afterward without hearing about hell-like experiences. Ring also noted that hell-like visions produced by drugs are not often repressed.[28]

These criticisms have some force, but they do not eliminate the fact that hell-like NDEs *are* reported—and not just by Rawlings, who is a Christian, but by others outside of biblical Christianity, such as Atwater. And even if reports of positive NDEs outnumber the negative accounts, this doesn't mean that hell-like experiences have nothing to say about objective reality. Majorities don't necessarily determine truth; after all, a majority of the world once believed the sun circled the earth.

D. Scott Rogo, a well-seasoned parapsychologist, noted that reactions to Rawlings were too severe, given that Rawlings's data was only anecdotal, as was Moody's original research. Rogo writes, "No matter how Dr. Rawlings came to collect his data, the fact remains that negative or hellish NDEs have now been placed on record by obviously sincere witnesses. . . Facts are facts, no matter how one comes by them."[29] Furthermore, any interpretation of the NDE ought to be able to account for these negative cases, and not simply dismiss them as irrelevant or imaginary.[30]

Psychologist Margot Grey—who, unlike Rawlings, does not hold a Christian view of the afterlife—agrees with Rawlings's claim that repression of a negative NDE may occur. She writes:

> From conversations with physicians who have re-counted to me cases of NDEs reported to them by their patients following resuscitation from clinical death and from my own research into the matter, I found evidence to support the claim that negative experiences are most likely to be obtained immediately after the event. This is due, so it seems, to the minimal time gap between the near-death episode

itself and the procuring of the information pertaining to it.[31]

Grey also agrees with Rawlings's observation that it is much less psychologically appealing to share a hellish NDE than to report a heavenly one. Ending up in torment instead of bliss is rather hard on one's self-esteem, and one would be less likely to share the news.[32] Nevertheless, some NDErs do recount hell-like experiences. Grey tells of one account that has a distinctively biblical ring to it:

> I was going down, down deep into the earth. There was anger and I felt this horrible fear. Everything was gray. The noise was fearsome, with snarling and crashing like maddened wild animals, gnashing their teeth.[33]

Grey, however, does not believe in a literal and eternal hell. She, like Atwater, claims that these experiences are not indicative of an objective state but of the subjective, internal condition of the NDEr. Using the language of Carl Jung and psychoanalysis, she says:

> I am inclined to feel that a more generalized archetypical interpretation is a possibility in cases of hell-like experiences where negative emotions have become trapped in the psyche and released during the near-death experience.[34]

Even if Grey and Atwater are right, and hell-like NDEs do not serve as evidence of hell itself, these experiences do tell us that all is not well in the human psyche. Grey recognizes that some people demonstrate a deep sense of guilt and unease about spiritual realities during their NDEs. This is no surprise from a

Christian perspective, since the Bible teaches that humans are pervasively affected by sin and have violated their consciences (Jeremiah 17:9; Romans 1–3).

However, as Rogo has pointed out, negative NDEs "represent experiences just as phenomenologically valid as classic [positive] NDEs." Moreover,

> people who suffer negative NDEs do not seem to be different psychologically from other near-death survivors. Nor does Dr. Grey take into account the fact that hellish NDEs emerge from the same initial stages (such as leaving the body and entering the darkness) which earmark classic NDEs. Her line of reasoning is a desperate attempt to recognize and bolster the good within the NDE while decrying and rejecting the bad.[35]

Despite Rogo's criticism of Grey's view regarding hell-like NDEs, he cautiously suggests explanations of his own; but these appear to have similar problems. He theorizes that hell-like NDEs are hallucinations caused by the trauma of violent resuscitation, that they are the result of drugs, or that they are merely vivid dreams.[36]

But negative NDEs were reported even before resuscitation techniques were available,[37] and many patients who experience violent resuscitations do not have negative experiences. It is also far from clear that the physical violence of the CPR procedure would translate into the protracted spiritual torment people endure in hell-like NDEs. Furthermore, most NDEs, whether negative or positive, are not explainable on the basis of drugs.[38] Lastly, if Rogo says that negative NDEs are merely the result of vivid dreams, he should say the same for positive NDEs experienced under similar conditions. Rogo wants to preserve the reality of the positive NDEs while explaining away the negative ones as subjective. In so doing, he seems to engage in the same kind of special pleading that he accuses Grey of committing.

Ring's viewpoint in *Life at Death*[39] and in two recent scholarly articles[40] also assumes the normality and reality of the positive NDEs and tries to explain away the negative ones as not representative of ultimate reality. When challenged on his interpretation of negative NDEs, Ring admitted that NDErs' reports are not in and of themselves adequate to explain the meaning of NDEs—whether positive or negative.[41] A larger frame of reference is needed in order to interpret the phenomena. Ring chooses to interpret NDEs on the basis of the pantheistic and monistic worldview taught in *A Course in Miracles*, which denies the ultimate reality of evil. He therefore concludes that the negative experiences are ultimately illusory.[42]

Although Atwater is reluctant to accept hell as a literal reality, she does state that "people who experience an unpleasant and/or hell-like near-death experience must be welcomed by researchers. . . . They have a lot to tell us."[43] And she admits that empirical "research facts cannot prove either claim" about the existence of heaven or hell.[44] Even Moody admitted in *Reflections on Life After Life* that "nothing I have encountered precludes the possibility of a hell."[45]

Atwater, Moody, and Ring are on to something significant. The accounts of NDEs cannot tell us everything we need to know about the afterlife. We need a reliable source of information from which to build or to fill out our explanations. Although Moody does not hold a biblical view of the NDE, he makes an excellent point when he argues that NDEs cannot refute the reality of the final judgment.

Some seem dissatisfied because they apparently think that these [near-death] experiences are inconsistent with the notion of a Final Judgment at the end of the world. I see no discrepancy here. Obviously, if anyone were to have come back from "death" reporting that he went through the Final Judgment, then his experience would have to be mistaken. Since the end of the world has not yet taken place, any report of its having occurred during a near-death experience would be, in effect, a disconfirmation of the validity of that experience. There may well be a Final Judgment; near-death experiences in no way imply the contrary.[46]

Although the Bible does not directly address NDEs,[47] it does speak clearly and repeatedly about the state immediately after irreversible death, as well as the ultimate state of the soul. Even if near-hell experiences cannot be verified, there is ample evidence in the teachings of Jesus Christ for dangers beyond the grave.

JESUS ON HEAVEN AND HELL

A stunning story about the afterlife is found in Luke's Gospel, chapter 16, where Jesus graphically describes two radically different destinies beyond death, one for a selfish rich man, the other for a poor beggar. The rich man ends up in agony and unthinkable torment; the beggar ends up comforted at "Abraham's side," in an afterlife of bliss. When the rich man cries out for some relief from the tormenting fires, Abraham tells him that "between us and you a great chasm has been fixed, so that those who want to go from here to you cannot, nor can anyone cross over from there to us" (Luke 16:26).

This story teaches that those favored by God will be carried to a blessed state after their death, and that the unrepentant will wind up in irreversible torment signified by the "agony of fire." Notice, too, that there is a great divide that cannot be bridged between these two states. Since the rich man's brothers were still alive on earth, this parable is speaking of the disembodied, intermediary state before the final resurrection of the just and the unjust (Daniel 12:1,2; Revelation 20:14). Nevertheless, it offers a dramatic portrayal of two very divergent destinies.[48] The apostle Peter affirms this when he says that "the Lord knows how to . . . keep the unrighteous under punishment until the day of judgment" (2 Peter 2:9 NRSV).

Jesus' parable about the weeds and the wheat (Matthew 13:24-30) also illustrates two contrasting and mutually exclusive destinies. The kingdom of God, he said, is like a man who sowed seed in his field. Yet while everyone slept, an enemy secretly came and planted weeds. When the bad seed sprouted, the farmer decided to let both wheat and weeds grow together until the harvest. Jesus explained that he is the sower of the good seed; the field is the world; the good seed represents the children of the kingdom; the weeds are the children of the evil one; the enemy who sows the bad seed is the devil; the harvest is the end of the world; the harvesters are angels. Having identified the references, Jesus drives home the point:

> As the weeds are pulled up and burned in the fire, so it will be at the end of the age. The Son of Man will send out his angels, and they will weed out of his kingdom everything that causes sin and all who do evil. They will throw them into the fiery furnace, where there will be weeping and gnashing of teeth. Then the righteous will shine like the sun in the kingdom of their Father. He who has ears, let him hear (Matthew 13:40-43,47-50).

The reference to "weeping and gnashing of teeth" graphically envokes the futile frustration of the hopeless ones, and it is reminiscent of the "snarling, crashing, and gnashing" NDE described above by Grey.

Jesus also compared his end-of-the-world separation of the righteous from the unrighteous to a shepherd who separates his sheep from the goats. Those who have served Christ will inherit the kingdom and eternal life, while those who have failed to serve Christ will be cursed and assigned to eternal punishment—which Jesus describes as "the eternal fire prepared for the devil and his angels" (Matthew 25:41). In this passage from Matthew's Gospel, the "eternal life" given to the righteous means everlasting fellowship with God and "eternal punishment" means everlasting separation from God. Both states are eternal in the same sense, for the same Greek word, *aionios*, is translated "eternal" in both cases.[49] Jesus also indicates that these are *conscious* eternal states. And, again, there is a great divide between these totally opposite destinies. No middle ground is offered; no hope of switching sides exists.

In his novel on this subject, *The Great Divorce*, C.S. Lewis noted that although the idea of a "marriage of heaven and hell" (to use the poet William Blake's phrase) is a perennial notion, it is nonetheless precisely the opposite of how reality works.

> We are not living in a world where all roads are radii of a circle and where all, if followed long enough, will therefore draw gradually nearer and finally meet at the centre: rather in a world where every road, after a few miles, forks into two, and each of those into two again, and at each fork you must make a decision. Even on this level, life is not like a pool but like a tree. It does not move toward unity but away from it. . . . Good, as it ripens, becomes continually

more different not only from evil but from other good.

I do not think that all who choose wrong roads perish; but their rescue consists in being put back on the right road.[50]

Jesus sought to rescue those on the wrong road by getting their feet on the right one. He cried, "Enter through the narrow gate. For wide is the gate and broad is the road that leads to destruction, and many enter through it" (Matthew 7:13). The gate leading to eternal life is Jesus himself. He said, "I am the gate; whoever enters through me will be saved. . . . The thief comes only to steal and kill and destroy; I have come that they may have life, and have it to the full" (John 10:9,10).

Jesus' images of the great divide—blessed Lazarus and the suffering rich man, the wheat and the weeds, the sheep and the goats, and the two roads—are graphic, unmistakable, and to the point. The picture Jesus paints of the afterlife leaves no room for a being of light who unconditionally accepts all people, whatever their "mistakes" or "ignorance" might be. This may make many people uncomfortable, but Jesus never accommodated his teaching to popular taste. And his audience recognized that he spoke with an authority that surpassed even the religious leaders (Matthew 7:28,29). Even if every hell-like NDE can be explained away, the reality of this great divide is anchored in the authority of Jesus himself.

THE HOLINESS OF GOD

The unbridgeable chasm between heaven and hell reflects the divide between God's holiness and human sinfulness—a divide that cannot be bridged through NDEs or human efforts at "being good," but only through God's offer of forgiveness through Jesus Christ's death and resurrection. Jesus said that he didn't come to call the religiously "righteous," but to summon sinners to repentance (Matthew 9:13). To the most scrupulous religious leaders of his time, Jesus said, "Not one of you keeps the law" (John 7:19). Jesus taught that the essence of God's moral law is to "love the Lord your God with all your heart and with all your soul and with all your mind. This is the first and greatest commandment" (Matthew 22:37,38). Whoever fails in this (namely, every one of us) fails to honor God and sins against God's holiness.

Jonathan Edwards (1703-58) emphasized our utter obligation to a holy God and the penalty of betraying our Sovereign:

> He is a Being of infinite greatness, majesty, and glory; and therefore he is infinitely honorable. He is infinitely exalted above the greatest potentates of the earth and highest angels in heaven; and therefore he is infinitely more honorable than they. His authority over us is infinite; and the ground of his right to our obedience is infinitely strong; for he is infinitely worthy to be obeyed himself and we have an absolute, universal, and infinite dependence upon him.[51]

Violating the sound moral advice of a parent, friend, or political leader pales in comparison to breaking the commandment of God himself, who is the sole source of all goodness and the absolute Governor of the universe. For this reason, theologian R.C. Sproul labels sin "cosmic treason."[52] Edwards agrees: "Sin against God, being a violation of infinite obligations, must be a crime infinitely heinous, and deserving of infinite punishment."[53]

God's perfect standard of goodness and our inability to keep it call into question Moody's explanation for why he hadn't run across accounts of hell. "The people I have interviewed have been normal, nice people," he said. Their "transgressions have been minor—the sorts of things we all have done." So "one would not expect that they would have been consigned to a fiery pit."[54]

Moody's cavalier attitude toward perdition underestimates both human sinfulness and divine holiness. The apostle Paul made the extent and reality of sin quite clear when he declared that "there is no one who does good, not even one," for "all have sinned and fall short of the glory of God" (Romans 3:12, 23). Moreover, "the wages of sin is death, but the gift of God is eternal life in Christ Jesus our Lord" (Romans 6:23).

The prophet Isaiah experienced the contrast between God's holiness and his own sin when God revealed both to him (Isaiah 6:1-7). He recounts what he would never forget in these words: "I saw the Lord seated on a throne, high and exalted, and the train of his robe filled the temple" (verse 1). God is depicted in the symbolism of respected royalty. He is enthroned in majesty. Isaiah then beheld worshiping angels (seraphs) who called out to each other, "Holy, holy, holy, is the LORD Almighty; the whole earth is full of his glory" (verse 3). At this angelic sound, "the doorposts and thresholds shook and the temple was filled with smoke" (verse 4).

Isaiah's response was not one of calm enjoyment or mystical ecstasy. He was shaking before the throne. "Woe to me!" he cried. "I am ruined! For I am a man of unclean lips, and I live among a people of unclean lips, and my eyes have seen the King, the LORD Almighty" (verse 5). Isaiah knew he was unworthy before the royal audience. There was no denying his own sin or the sins of his people, even though they were a people of God's own choosing. The inescapable and omnipresent holiness of God was a crushing indictment of the unholiness of Isaiah and of all Israel.

The moral rift between Isaiah and the thrice-holy God was

only resolved through God's intervention after Isaiah's repentant cry. One of the angels took a live coal from God's altar and touched Isaiah's mouth with it, saying, "See ... your guilt is taken away and your sin atoned for" (verse 7; see also Leviticus 16:12). Forgiveness and restoration come from the throne of a holy God—on his terms.[55]

Betty Eadie, on the other hand, claims that during her NDE she was told that the heavenly realm doesn't see sin in this way, but merely as a breaking of the laws of nature. Sin does not result in eternal separation from God, but merely in a forfeiture of the good things that would otherwise have accrued to our benefit.[56] Eadie insists that Jesus "never wanted to do or say anything that would offend me."[57] Like most NDErs, she says nothing about sinning against a "holy, holy, holy" God. Holiness does not appear to be a category in Eadie's thinking about God, Jesus, and the afterlife.[58]

HEAVEN AND HELL REVISITED

Whether positive or negative, NDEs cannot by themselves tell us about the *ultimate* state of a person's soul, due to their short duration, contradictory natures, and lack of finality. The reality of hell-like NDEs, however, hints that all may not be well for everyone on the other side. The near-hell experience may be a foretaste of hell itself—rather like a "coming attraction" at the movies. Though the negative accounts vary (some being closer to the biblical concept of divine punishment than others), they may well serve as a warning.

Sixth-century historian and bishop St. Gregory of Tours considered this to be a distinct possibility:

> In His unbounded mercy, the good God allows some
> souls to return to their bodies shortly after death, so
> that the sight of hell might at last teach them to fear

the eternal punishments in which words alone could not make them believe.[59]

Maurice Rawlings, who has been "involved in reviewing emergency situations and sudden deaths for three and a half decades,"[60] noted that in the rare instances in which an individual clinically dies and has a bad NDE, and then clinically dies at some later point and has another NDE, the second NDE is invariably a good one. The significance of this, in Rawlings's view, is that "there's nothing like a little bit of hell to dramatically change [one's] life's purpose and attitude."[61]

Mark Sheehan, a Denver cardiologist and a Christian, reported a startling NDE to me. Gene, a man with a history of heart problems, went into cardiac arrest while Dr. Sheehan was examining him. After he was resuscitated, Gene looked directly at Sheehan and cried, "I'm not going up there!" Dr. Sheehan drew close and asked what he meant. He replied, "I saw Jesus standing next to you. But Jesus did not know me or accept me! What do I do?" At this, Dr. Sheehan prayed with the man to repent of his sins and to receive Christ as Savior and Lord. Gene died shortly after this, and his wife reported that he was at "peace with the Lord."[62]

Such cases may indeed bear witness to the ancient but timeless words of St. Gregory.

6

BELIEFS OF THE NEAR-DEAD

*Between heaven and hell is only this life, which is the
most fragile thing in the world.*

—Blaise Pascal

The person who has had an NDE is usually profoundly affected
by it. As we have seen, researchers find that an NDE tends to
lead to a diminished fear of death and a renewed zest for life. It
can also create or intensify spiritual interests, or alter one's
worldview or beliefs.

But what new beliefs are likely to be taken on board? What
spiritual views about God, creation, human beings, salvation,
death, and the afterlife usually follow in the wake of an NDE?
Answers to such questions can be found by looking at what the
NDErs, the "spirit beings," and the researchers have to say.

CHILDREN OF A VAGUE GOD?

In *The Light Beyond*, Raymond Moody states that NDEs
challenge traditional religious understandings. He maintains
that whether or not NDErs were religious before their NDE,
they usually

> emerge with an appreciation of religion that is differ-
> ent from the narrowly defined one established by most

churches. They come to realize through this experience that religion is not a matter of one "right" group
versus several "wrong" groups. People who undergo
an NDE come out of it saying that religion concerns
your ability to love—not doctrine and denominations. In short, they think that God is a much more
magnanimous being than they previously thought,
and that denominations don't count.[1]

This is almost identical to Betty Eadie's experience. After
receiving "knowledge" from the being of light she calls Jesus,
she then "knew that we have no right to criticize any church or
any religion in any way."[2]

This claim means that we ought to refrain from rebuking
wayward churches that, for example, teach their members to
withhold medical treatment from a dying child. Should we
not correct a religious sect if it teaches that people who are
dark-skinned are inferior to whites?[3] The Jesus of the New
Testament created his strongest enemies by criticizing their
"religion," and his criticisms were on target (Luke 23). One
scholar notes that because of Jesus' "loyalty to the truth, He
was not afraid to dissent publicly from official doctrines (if He
knew they were wrong), to expose error, and to warn His disciples of false teachers."[4]

Moody tells of a man who had been "a minister of the fire
and brimstone variety" who frequently warned his congregation that if "they didn't believe the Bible in a certain way,
they would be condemned to burn eternally."[5] During this
man's NDE, the being of light told him, in a nondemanding
way, not to speak to his congregation about hell anymore because it was making them miserable. After this experience, the
pastor preached messages of love instead of fear.[6] Similarly, a
"doctrine-abiding Lutheran" woman had an NDE and was
afterward convinced that her God was not concerned with

"church doctrine at all."[7] Moody also quotes Kenneth Ring as saying, "the basic message of the NDE" is that "knowledge and love are the most important things. It is the formal religions that have added the dogma and doctrine."[8]

In *Closer to the Light*, Melvin Morse records the story of a 43-year-old woman who had undergone an NDE at age nine after nearly drowning. This woman now has "only a vague conception of God" and has dabbled in many religions.[9] Her NDE was not deep but fragmentary. Yet she says that "from my brief encounter, I got the idea that being one with God is something that can be done without rules," and that "the rules of religion are put there by people."[10]

There is a trace of truth in her remark. The Bible warns against people corrupting God's Word through the accumulation of merely human traditions (Matthew 15:1-9). However, "without rules"—that is, without a developed, specific, and trustworthy theology—no one could ever know for certain what God is like or what is required by him in order for us to honor him. It would all be left to guesswork, which is the upshot of many remarks that Moody and other researchers have heard from NDErs. After their NDE, many have opted for a vague notion of God, spiritual knowledge without clear guidelines, and love without absolute moral demands.

Such a "theology" is troublesome. If God desires us to know him and to love one another, but if we are not accurately taught how to do this, then we could easily get it all wrong. It is not enough to base one's understanding of the nature of God and the practice of love merely on private likes, dislikes, and preferences. The outcome is bound to be contradictory.[11] Is it "loving" to abort a handicapped unborn child, or is it "loving" to bring it into the world? Affirming that we should be "loving" doesn't answer this question at all, since people on both sides of the issue advocate conflicting choices as the "loving" thing to do.[12]

THE NEW AGE EMPHASIS

Even NDErs who set traditional religious views aside may still adopt a particular theology or doctrine. Well-known consciousness researcher Stanislov Grof believes that:

> The core NDE is a powerful catalyst of spiritual awakening and conscious evolution. Its long-term aftereffects include . . . [a] more open attitude toward reincarnation and [the] development of [a] universal spirituality that transcends divisive interests of religious sectarians and resembles the best of the mystical traditions of the great Oriental philosophies.[13]

Many mystical traditions, especially those of the Orient, are not founded on monotheism (belief in one personal God who is distinct from his creation). They are generally based on monism (all is one) and pantheism (all is God). Remarks from NDErs quite often express a nonmonotheistic worldview. Consider, for example, one NDEr's description:

> I knew it was God. . . . There is no doubt in my mind that it was God. God was me and I was God. I was part of the light and I was one with it. I was not separate. I am not saying that I am a supreme being. I was God, as you are, as everyone is.[14]

This man's NDE encouraged him to adopt a pantheistic view of God. He now believes that God is everything and everyone; God is not a personal Lord over creation but a divine spiritual principle or force that permeates all things. This has a lot in common with New Age thought and certain schools of Hinduism, Buddhism, and Taoism; but it is alien to Christianity.

Dannion Brinkley, who claims to have died twice (each involving an extended NDE), says that during his first NDE, the being of light said, "Who you are is the difference that God makes. . . . And that difference is love." Brinkley "is not sure of the exact meaning of this cryptic phrase."[15] But pantheism seems to be in mind. At a later point, he says that when you control the energy of the body "and transform it into a positive force, you have found that part of you that is God."[16]

In *Heading Toward Omega*, Kenneth Ring tells of a woman who was raised a Protestant, rejected it, researched Catholicism, and rejected it as well. She became, in her words, "a ranting, raving atheist." But now, after her NDE, she says she knows beyond question that there is a God, and "that God is everything that exists, [that's] the essence of God. . . . Everything that exists has the essence of God with it."[17] A similar view is offered by another NDEr, who emphasizes the immanence of God:

> I think of God as a tremendous source of energy, like the nucleus of something enormous and that we are all just separate atoms from this nucleus. I think that God is in every one of us; we are God.[18]

P.M.H. Atwater, who claims to have died three times in 1977, echoes this view of God. She says that through her NDEs she "found that we never left the God we thought we lost because *God is all that is*."[19]

The belief that God is an all-encompassing energy or reality usually includes the idea that God is not a distinct, personal being (as monotheistic religions teach); rather, "God" is an impersonal force, principle, or consciousness. For instance, Ring recounts an NDEr who said:

> The next sensation is this wonderful, wonderful feeling of this light. . . . It's almost like a person. It is *not* a person, but it is a being of some kind. It is a

mass of energy. It doesn't have a character like you
would describe another person, but it has a character
in that it is more than just a thing.[20]

Another NDEr remembered being peacefully drawn like a
magnet to a white light. "There was no face in the light like
some people describe. I didn't see God or anything. It was
more like energy, and it was very wonderful."[21]

In summarizing his research on the effects of the NDE, Ring
stated that those who experience the light are infused with it
"so as to lead to a complete union with the light," which means
that NDErs "may experience [a] merging of their own individ-
uality with the divine."[22]

Belief in the unity or oneness of being (monism) is often
associated with belief in the divinity of all things (pantheism).
The idea of the oneness of being is frequently apparent in NDErs'
accounts of their experiences. One woman said that during her
NDE she gazed upon a "golden light" that did not burn her
eyes; rather, she gained strength from gazing upon it.

> It's as if by gazing upon this beautiful golden light
> the power that it was was revitalizing something
> within the depths of me. There was a transmission
> of a higher power, knowledge, understanding, and
> the "oneness of being" through gazing upon the
> light.[23]

This concept is an essential aspect of many Oriental and
occult belief systems. Instead of seeing God as a personal
being who transcends the universe he created and sustains,
pantheistic monism teaches that there is no ultimate distinction between God and the universe, or between different things
in the universe. God is not separate from the universe, nor is
anything in the universe separate from anything else. All is
one and one is all, and everything is divine.

The fundamental human problem, therefore, is not sin; it is ignorance and false perception. We fail to perceive that "all is one" because we are unenlightened. The above NDE account speaks of a higher power, a "golden light" that revitalized something within this woman and thereby dispelled her ignorance about being "one" with all things. In this sense, the NDE can produce the same result as many New Age "psychotechnologies" (such as yoga or visualization), to use Marilyn Ferguson's term.[24]

Ring tells of a letter he received from a woman who described how her NDE changed her worldview. She wrote that "there is a deeper love and unity with everyone and everything that I come in contact with. I seem to have a greater awareness of all living things and that we are ALL a part of one another and ultimately part of a greater consciousness, God."[25]

Eadie speaks of an experience during her NDE in which she and a rose and everything else were one.[26] She also mentions having always been a part of Jesus.[27] These remarks sound pantheistic (being part of Jesus) and monistic (being one with everything); however, she also sometimes speaks of God in personal terms as a being who is distinct from angels and humans. But in general, Eadie gravitates toward pantheism and monism when she asserts the centrality and power of the self. "All healing comes from within. All misery comes from within. We can create our own spiral of despair, or we can create a trampoline of happiness and attainment. Our thoughts have *tremendous* power."[28] She tends to view God as an impersonal power source that can be tapped into:

> We can recharge our own spirits through serving others, having faith in God, and simply opening ourselves to positive energy through positive thoughts. *We* control it. The source of energy is God and is always there, but we must tune him in. We must

accept the power of God if we want to enjoy the
effects of it in our lives.[29]

Any concept of God as an impersonal force or energy has no
place in the Christian worldview. For instance, the Bible never
implies that we can "tune in" to God, as if he were a cosmic
radio wave. But the notion that a universal divine power is
available for us to "plug into" pervades our culture. It is found,
for example, in the *Star Wars* movies, children's Saturday
morning cartoons, and diverse New Age teachings. It is also a
belief fairly common among NDErs.[30]

BEYOND SIN

Another non-Christian belief derived from many NDEs is
that we should not be concerned about sin in the sense of the
Bible's concept of moral wrongdoing, which includes idolatry,
adultery, fornication, murder, lying, stealing, being covetous,
taking revenge, and so on. One NDEr said to the being she
encountered, "This is all so beautiful, this is all so perfect,
what about my sins?" To this the being replied, "There are no
sins. Not in the way you think about them on earth. The only
thing that matters here is how you think."[31] Upon hearing this
the woman "knew that everything, everywhere in the universe
was OK, that the plan was perfect. That whatever was happening—the wars, famine, whatever—was OK."[32] Sin, pain,
misery, and tragedy seem to have been eliminated from her
worldview. Eadie likewise reports that sins are viewed differently—that is, less severely—in the spiritual realm.[33]

Such a perspective dulls or eliminates the sting of sin and
evil, and embraces a kind of Pollyanna theology that excludes
real tragedy. In a tear-stained world shocked and saddened
by desperate refugees, bloody tribalism, rape, child abuse,
abortion-on-demand, drug addiction, and all manner of ills,

there is good reason to question such postmortem "wisdom." The biblical view of God's providence differs from pantheistic, monistic religions in that it affirms the reality of evil as well as the inability of evil ultimately to thwart God's sovereign design for history (Genesis 50:20; Ephesians 1:11).

Moody mentions that many NDErs exchanged the "reward-punishment model" of a last judgment for one of "cooperative development toward the ultimate end of self-realization."[34] Eadie's experience also caused her to abandon the harsh God of her youth and to embrace a Christ that accepts everyone.

Advocates of these NDE perspectives fail to see that the biblical view is neither a "reward-punishment model" nor a "self-realization model," but a "grace-punishment model."[35] One receives eternal life and avoids eternal punishment through accepting the grace of God demonstrated in Jesus Christ. Paul taught that "when the kindness and love of God our Savior appeared, he saved us, not because of righteous things we had done, but because of his mercy" (Titus 3:4,5; see also Ephesians 2:8,9).

ARE ALL RELIGIONS ONE?

Many NDErs come to view all religions as having an underlying unity. They believe the historically divergent and competitive religions should be replaced with one universal faith. As one NDEr put it, "All religions started from the same truth and there is little variation between the major beliefs of each." He goes on to express his yearning for a new ecumenical faith: "What a great tool this will be to at least begin to unify mankind under one God, one truth and one spiritual belief."[36]

But there is neither theological nor historical justification for the notion that all religions "started from the same truth," nor does this romantic theory account for why so little agreement exists between religions today on the titanic issues of God, humanity, salvation, and the afterlife.[37] Nonetheless, many NDErs have been encouraged by their experiences to abandon traditional religious antagonisms in favor of an orientally flavored universalism and syncretism.[38]

Morse claims that "many of the world's great religious leaders have been driven by profound near-death and other visionary experiences that involve the mystical light."[39] This would make many religions dependent on the same basic experience, and it would support the idea of the essential unity of different religions despite their stated doctrinal differences. It would, however, exclude Christianity, which is based on the historical life, death, and resurrection of Jesus Christ, not on someone's mystical experience.[40]

REINCARNATION

One belief common to Oriental religions but absent from the monotheistic religions (Judaism, Christianity, and Islam) is reincarnation, which is the idea that the soul has many embodiments throughout history. Ring's first study, *Life at Death*, suggested that NDErs were more likely than non-NDErs to be open to the idea of reincarnation. Ring did not mean that all NDErs converted to the belief. Some did; others just took it more seriously. His second study confirmed this, but he noted that "the average belief in reincarnation was still quite moderate."[41]

Atwater's impression was that "reincarnation is a favorite topic for near-death survivors. . . . For most, it becomes a fact of life."[42] According to Atwater, a number of NDErs claim to have experienced previous lifetimes during their NDEs, and many believe that one lifetime is not enough to perfect "The Self" within them on "its journey back to The One True

Source of All."[43] In other words, it takes many lifetimes to fully realize one's divinity (pantheism).

The Bible teaches that humans will never realize their divinity because they are not God; they are created by God (Genesis 1:26,27). The holiness of God and the corruption of humans makes it impossible to obtain salvation by working out one's karma; for, according to Paul, no one shall be justified before God by observing the moral law (Galatians 3:11). Justification before a holy God comes only when the perfect righteousness of Christ is accredited to a person, despite that person's sin. This is a gift that can be received only through faith in the work of Jesus Christ (Romans 3–5; Galatians 3–4).

Reincarnation denies the sufficiency of Christ's sinless sacrifice for sin, since it teaches that we must work out our own karma through repeated lifetimes. To this, the writer of Hebrews says:

> He has appeared once for all at the end of the age to remove sin by the sacrifice of himself. And just as it is appointed for mortals to die once, and after that the judgment, so Christ, having been offered once to bear the sins of many, will appear a second time, not to deal with sin, but to save those who are eagerly waiting for him (Hebrews 9:26-28 NRSV).

Furthermore, the biblical doctrine of the resurrection of the body at the end of history (Daniel 12:1,2; 1 Corinthians 15:12-58) contradicts the idea of successive reincarnations.[44]

APPARITIONS OF THE DEAD

Moody's most recent book, *Reunions: Visionary Encounters with Departed Loved Ones* (1993), indicates another way in which NDEs affect or alter beliefs: through encouraging a spiritistic or occult view of reality. The appearance of what many take to be dead relatives is fairly common during NDEs. Moody wanted to duplicate this aspect of the NDE so that he could contact departed loved ones without having to die himself.[45] Based on his research into the occult practice of necromancy (a method of contacting the dead), Moody built a special kind of seance chamber that he called the "psychomanteum," after the ancient Greek oracles of the dead. This "apparition chamber" has a comfortable chair placed three feet in front of a large mirror. The chair is tilted so that a person gazing into the mirror sees only the reflection of a black velvet curtain. The room is faintly illuminated by a stained-glass lamp with a 15-watt bulb.

Moody tested his seance chamber with ten subjects who were interested in contacting the dead. After spending a day with these people, Moody admitted them—along with their mementos of deceased relatives—into his psychomanteum. According to Moody, five of the ten people experienced their desired apparitions, and he himself was able to contact his grandmother through the process.[46]

Such adventures indicate a connection between the NDE and the worldview of spiritism or spiritualism—the belief that the dead are within our perceptual reach, whether through a medium or a more direct access. The heyday of spiritualism in America occurred during the mid-to-late nineteenth century, but these beliefs have endured and seem to be reviving.[47]

Other researchers have also noted the similarities between the beliefs of NDErs and of spiritualism. D. Scott Rogo, an authority on the paranormal, observed, "I cannot help but be impressed by how closely the findings of everyone from [Karlis] Osis to [Raymond] Moody match what the Spiritualists of the Victorian age taught about death and the process of dying."[48] The major points of similarity include the belief in life after death, the benign nature of the afterlife, and the ability of the living to contact the dead.

In contrast to spiritualism, biblical Christianity rejects contact with the dead in favor of a relationship with the living God, who has revealed to us all that we need to know through the biblical record of his witnesses, whether prophets, apostles, or Jesus Christ himself. The dead are in God's hands and are not to be summoned back.[49] Isaiah the prophet warned:

> When they say to you, "Seek those who are mediums and wizards, who whisper and mutter," should not a people seek their God? Should they seek the dead on behalf of the living? To the law and to the testimony! If they do not speak according to this word, it is because there is no light in them (Isaiah 8:19,20 NKJV; see also Deuteronomy 18:10-12; 2 Chronicles 33:6).

Likewise, the apostle Paul said that "idolatry and witchcraft" (which includes necromancy) are "acts of the sinful nature" and not fruit of the Holy Spirit (Galatians 5:19-23; see also Revelation 21:7,8; 22:14,15).

WHO OR WHAT IS THE LIGHT?

So far we have seen that NDEs can foster a pantheistic, monistic, syncretistic, occultic, or spiritualistic worldview. These worldviews differ significantly from Christianity. However, some NDErs have encountered a being of light whom they describe as very much like Jesus Christ himself.

Dan was an active homosexual who had contracted gonorrhea and was being treated with a massive dose of antibiotics, which triggered anaphylactic shock. With no heartbeat and a flat electrocardiogram, Dan saw himself lying on the floor amidst the activities of the doctors and nurses who were trying to revive him. He then traveled through a dark tunnel to a beautiful garden, hedged by a fence that stopped him from going further. A brilliant light appeared, radiating love and peace, and Dan knew it was Jesus Christ. Yet this being of light was not all-accepting. Sin was indeed a problem, for Dan heard the words, "It is not time to come into my Father's kingdom. You have not lived as I intended. Go back and glorify me." Dan returned to his body and awoke as a follower of Jesus Christ. He stopped his homosexual ways and became part of a devoted Christian community.[50]

One woman, after being struck by lightning on a camping trip, encountered the glory of God and became panic-stricken. She describes her experience:

> At this point in the act of dying, I had what I call the answer to a question I had never verbalized to anyone or even faced: Is there really a God? I can't describe it, but the totality and reality of the Living God exploded within my being and He filled every atom of my body with His glory. In the next moment, to my horror, I found that I wasn't going toward God. I was going away from Him. It was like seeing what might have been, but going away from it. In my panic, I started trying to communicate with the God I knew was there.[51]

She begged God to spare her life and offered it to him if she were to live. In three months she had recovered fully.[52]

Although this account doesn't identify Jesus Christ or tell what the woman did with her life after recovering, her NDE resonates with the biblical theme that human beings in their own goodness are not worthy of God's sinless presence. The apostle Paul said that those "who do not know God and do not obey the gospel of our Lord Jesus . . . will be punished with everlasting destruction and shut out from the presence of the Lord and from the majesty of his power" (2 Thessalonians

1:8,9). This woman may have had a preview of the horror of eternal separation from God.

On the other hand, some NDErs claim to have had previews of heaven. Maurice Rawlings reports:

> Many of my patients are Christians, and the glimpse of glory [seen in the NDE] seems so real, God so near, that they want to recount the event to any cooperative listener. There is no ambiguity. They identify this brilliant "being" as Christ himself. No question of counterfeit.[53]

All researchers and NDErs, however, do not identify the being of light with Jesus. Moody thinks that the deep NDE always involves a being of light, but he recognizes that the "identification of the being varies from individual to individual and seems to be largely a function of the religious background, training, or beliefs of the person involved."[54] Ring maintains that the light does not always appear as a "being," but he agrees with Moody that it represents a basic divine reality that is variously interpreted.[55] Characterizing the light as always divine is problematic, however, because of the diverse and contradictory ways in which people describe, understand, and respond to it.[56]

Consider the following. Ring records a strange NDE in which the being of light told a woman "who had been raised in the Fundamentalist tradition" that she was really Jewish. She didn't identify the being as Jesus Christ, yet she began a search for her identity, which included converting to Judaism, divorcing her husband, and abandoning her shy ways to become active in politics.[57] This account contradicts Michael Sabom's findings that the NDE does not cause people to switch religions (see chapter 4). It is also evidence of the diversity and unpredictability of the NDE and its effects.

Sometimes atheists who have NDEs remain atheists. One outstanding case is that of distinguished atheist philosopher A.J. Ayer, a leader of a philosophy called logical positivism, which dismisses as meaningless anything not empirically verifiable through scientific means. In an article entitled "What I Saw When I Was Dead," Ayer recounted his surprising NDE. While recovering from pneumonia, Ayer choked on a piece of food and was clinically dead for about four minutes. He remembered being "confronted by a red light, exceedingly bright and also very painful even when I turned away from it." He also recalled being "aware that this light was responsible for the government of the universe."[58]

Despite this remarkable occurrence, Ayer questioned whether it served as evidence of the soul's existence apart from the body. He reasoned that, because the stopping of the heart may not entail the arresting of brain function, "the most probable hypothesis is that my brain continued to function although my heart had stopped."[59] Ayer concluded:

> My recent experiences have slightly weakened my conviction that my genuine death, which is due fairly soon, will be the end of me, though I continue to hope that it will be. They have not weakened my conviction that there is no god. I hope my remaining an atheist will allay the anxieties of my fellow supporters of the Humanist Association, the Rationalist Press, and the South Place Ethical Society.[60]

In good British tradition, Ayer was wry to the end. Apparently the light "responsible for the government of the universe" didn't make much of a philosophical impression on him. His NDE was minimal compared to some, since it lacked such elements as the tunnel, the life-review, intense feelings of peace, visions of deceased relatives (or philosophers!), and communication with the light. Ayer died shortly after the article was published.

Other NDErs encounter a brilliant being but do not identify it as God. A woman who had had an NDE as a child said, "Others have seen God, but I only saw a Light, a Light that I will never forget."[61] Another woman was quite insistent that her NDE at age 15 did not reveal God, although she says she felt "warm and comfortable" and that her "body was illuminated by Light."[62] Now 44 years old, this woman says her NDE made her "more tolerant of other people's beliefs." She believes in reincarnation, but not in God. "For me this experience proved that there is life immediately after death. My experience didn't show me a god, so I can't really believe in one."[63]

MAKING SENSE OF IT ALL

Readers hoping to find a consistent message from NDEs may have found both this chapter and the previous one disturbing. Despite some structural commonalities, NDEs do not deliver a consistent message on the great questions about God, life, death, and spiritual liberation. Some NDErs experience hell or something hell-like; others find messages compatible with Oriental religions or spiritualism; others discover a Christ-filled bliss or even a word of rebuke from Jesus. Some return and remain atheists; others switch religions or become more religious. Clearly, there is no unified chorus being sung by those returning from clinical death.

What, then, should we believe about our forever? Numerous questions continue to haunt us. What kind of death do NDErs actually experience? Have they truly visited "the other side"? And what is the significance of the NDE for the living?

7

Do They Really Die?

Reports of my death have been greatly exaggerated.
—Mark Twain

There is no question that the near-death experience is functioning for many people as a new revelation about the afterlife and spiritual reality. Bruce Greyson, editor of the *Journal of Near-Death Studies*, is very optimistic. "Thanks to medical technology," he says, "the NDE may become our most common doorway to spiritual development."[1] If so, studying NDEs might one day vie with traditional religious activities—such as prayer, meditation, Bible study, worship, and loving service—as a popular means of spiritual growth.

How then do we evaluate the truthfulness of NDErs' claims, especially when differing and even contradictory experiences seem intensely real to the people themselves? Can we rely on these reports for information about the afterlife? What does the NDE signify about spiritual reality?

As we have seen, Michael Sabom has been able to verify the out-of-the-body experience (OBE) that occurs in some NDEs. However, the "transcendental NDE"—which includes such elements as the light, spirit beings, and a life-review—is not subject to the same kind of test. Although transcendental NDEs show a consistent structural pattern and are perceived to be as real as empirically verifiable OBEs, there is "no way to corroborate the details reported in these experiences, as has been done with the autoscopic [or OBE aspect of the] NDE."[2]

NDEs would probably be less spiritually fascinating and controversial without the notion that those who have "died" and returned are in a unique position to know and explain to the rest of us what it is like on "the other side." The "authority" of the NDE as a source of information about the nature of the afterlife rests on the assumption that NDErs have actually passed beyond death's door and then returned. But have they? Has any person who claims to have had an NDE actually died? Did Betty Eadie really die, for example?

THREE DEATHS

If we are to understand what the NDE tells us about the ultimate issues of death and the afterlife, we must understand the nature of death. In *Life After Life*, Moody gives three definitions of human death. The first describes death as "the absence of clinically detectable vital signs," such as breathing, heartbeat, and blood pressure, which is accompanied by dilation of the pupils and decrease in body temperature.[3] This definition is called "clinical death," and it allows for resuscitation because the patient's condition is reversible. Moody notes that "in order for resuscitation to have occurred, some degree of residual biological activity must have been going on in the cells of the body, even though the overt signs of these processes were not clinically detectable."[4] Because of the resulting brain damage, it is rare for anyone to be resuscitated after more than five or six minutes of clinical death.[5]

Another definition of death is the "lack of brain wave activity."[6] This covers cases in which the rest of the physical organism functions while the electroencephalograph (EEG) machine fails to detect any electrical activity in the brain. In many medical emergencies there is no time to find out whether

NDErs are experiencing brain-wave activity, so it is difficult to know what, if any, electrical activity occurs during the NDE. The EEG is also far from infallible. However, people with flat EEG readings have been resuscitated. Drawing from an 18-year study of NDEs, cardiologist Fred Schoonmaker reported in 1979 that about 55 NDEs involved flat EEG readings.[7]

Moody's third understanding of death is "the irreversible loss of vital functions."[8] By definition, no one can be resuscitated from this state of *biological* death[9]—although the Bible records several instances of people who were miraculously brought back from biological death by the power of God.[10] Also, what might have been clinical death in one set of circumstances could have been biological death in another. If, for example, Sam's heart stops beating while he is alone at the beach, it is unlikely that he will revive by himself. If his heart stops beating while he's in the hospital, it is possible that he will be resuscitated. Moody and others have said that it is impossible to know when one has reached the point of no return, biologically speaking, for it varies from person to person.

If someone returns from clinical death with an account of life beyond, what are we to make of it? We only know one thing for sure so far: The person is describing a "life" beyond clinical death but *before* biological death. Although it is difficult to say just how close to irreversible death any particular NDEr may have been, Moody is right to point out that bona fide NDErs "have been much closer to [death] than have the vast majority of their fellow human beings. . . . [So] I am quite willing to listen to what they have to say."[11]

NEAR-DEATH EXPERIENCES WITH AND WITHOUT CLINICAL DEATH

To complicate matters, NDEs have been purported to occur

before the point of clinical death.[12] There appear to be what
P.M.H. Atwater calls "near-death-like experiences," which involve NDE elements (either positive or negative) in the absence
of clinical death.[13] Some people mistake their experiences as
having occurred during clinical death when, in fact, they occurred while they were still alive. In one study of 40 patients
who had reported NDE symptoms, it was found that while 33
(82.5 percent) believed they had been "dead" or near death,
only 18 (45 percent) had experienced serious life-threatening
illnesses or injuries. For 22 (55 percent) of the patients, the
medical records showed no life-threatening conditions. Though
problems in the medical records could account for some of the
discrepancies, it is likely that the belief that one is dying is
an "important precipitator of the so-called near-death experience."[14] This has cleverly been called the "fear-death
experience."[15] The study concluded that although NDE researchers Michael Sabom and Melvin Morse provided records on
the medical conditions of a series of NDE patients, it "appeared
. . . that a considerable literature about these experiences rested
on uncorroborated statements of patients."[16]

The results of an unofficial 1992 questionnaire that was dis-
tributed to members of the International Association for Near-
Death Studies indicated that of the 229 who claimed to have
experienced the NDE phenomenon, only 23 percent had done
so during clinical death. Forty percent claimed to have had an
NDE during a serious illness or trauma, while 37 percent were
nowhere near death during their "neardeath experience"![17]
These findings contradict Melvin Morse's claim that one must
clinically die in order to have the experiences associated with
the NDE. Apparently his sample was too limited.[18]

Along similar lines, the findings of George Gallup's *Adventures in Immortality* (1982) are often cited to show the prevalence of NDEs. Gallup's poll asked this question: "Have you,
yourself, ever been on the verge of death or had a 'close call'

which involved any unusual experience at that time?"[19] Fifteen percent answered in the affirmative. In 1982, Gallup calculated this to mean eight million Americans. Although this figure is often thrown around (and adjusted for the present population),[20] it is far from accurate in assessing how many people have actually had NDEs because these figures were based only on people's perceptions with no corroboration from medical records.

Reports of brushes with death can be unintentionally fabricated. The Gallup question concerning "a close call" with death is ambiguous. This could mean either *being* medically close to death (such as in cardiac arrest) or simply *perceiving* oneself to be near death (such as fearing an imminent car crash or overestimating the severity of a medical condition).[21]

In a survey of 1000 university students, 107 said they had come close to death. Yet half of these had only faced a *potential* danger, which they had avoided. After these were excluded from the study, the researchers addressed only the 32 students who had become unconscious. Of these, only seven had experienced an NDE. This translates to only 0.7 percent—a figure far removed from Gallup's 15 percent! This study indicated that a bona fide NDE is probably much rarer than is generally believed.[22] To adapt a witticism from Mark Twain, the reports of some NDErs' deaths have been greatly exaggerated.

The upshot is that if the NDE is to function as a firsthand report about the afterlife, it must at least occur during clinical death. Extraordinary experiences occurring *before* clinical death, no matter how much they resemble a genuine NDE, cannot qualify as firsthand reports of what happens to people who are clinically dead.

Furthermore, since clinical-death NDEs *are* quite similar to pre-death "NDEs" (which could not possibly be experiences of the afterlife, whatever else they may be), then perhaps the NDEs that occur during clinical death are not experiences of the

afterlife either. Perhaps both phenomena are merely limited
explorations of the spirit world by a soul temporarily outside of
the body. Such visits to the spirit realm are not necessarily the
same thing as being permanently and irrevocably assigned to
an afterlife of either heaven or hell.

While Dannion Brinkley was recuperating from his clinical
death, he claims that by dreaming he entered the same spiritual world that he had visited during his NDE—although he
says that in his dreams, unlike during his NDE, he was aware
of his physical body.[23] If this place to which he journeyed was
the afterlife, how could he have gone back and forth between
this life and the next, all the while being physically in this life?
By definition, the afterlife is just that: where people go *after*
this life, not *during* it. How could any place that people visit
during this life be the *after*life? If the spiritual realm that is
visited in near-death-like experiences is more or less the same
spiritual realm that is visited during clinical death, then people
who have NDEs may not be experiencing the afterlife at all.

HOW MUCH LIKE DEATH IS
THE NEAR-DEATH EXPERIENCE?

To interpret the NDE as a first taste of what everyone experiences after death is to go beyond the evidence. Even if
Betty Eadie and other NDErs encountered an unconditionally
accepting being of light during clinical death, they may well
see nothing of such a being when they finally do die and enter
the afterlife. After all, those who have come back from the
edge of death to report an NDE were only *near* death; they
were not in the final state of biological death.

But what concerns most of us is our ultimate fate after biological death. Since our bodies return to the dust, what will
happen to our souls? Is there anything experienced during the
state of clinical death that is relevant to this question?

We know that a genuine NDE is a rare conscious experience during clinical death that cannot be adequately explained according to physical factors alone. However, the only thing this establishes is what Habermas and Moreland call a "minimalistic view of life after death,"[24] which means that when the soul is separated from the body during clinical death, it continues to exist for a short period of time. The NDE cannot tell us how much longer the soul will exist, or the conditions under which it will exist.

Whatever may happen during an NDE is of a minimal duration and is not the final state. This is why it is called a *near*-death experience. Sabom concludes his study of NDEs by answering the question, "Does the NDE represent a glimpse of an afterlife?"

> As a physician and a scientist, I cannot, of course, say for sure that the NDE is indicative of what is to come at the moment of *final* bodily death. These experiences were encountered during waning moments of life. Those reporting these experiences were *not brought back from the dead*, but were rescued from a point *very close to death*. Thus, in the strictest sense, these experiences are encounters of *near*-death, and not of death itself.[25]

Many NDEs involve the awareness of a barrier or divide that one cannot cross and still return to the body.[26] This may symbolize at least one difference between near-death and final death, although some NDErs claim to have crossed over and to have come back.[27] Atwater states, "It is of importance to me that no near-death survivor has ever described a *total* release or disconnection from his or her body."[28] Some NDErs mention the soul being sucked back into the body upon resuscitation, which implies some manner of connection between the two. The soul returns when the body is ready.

Both NDErs and those who have had OBEs without NDEs sometimes speak of a cord connecting the soul to the body. This phenomenon is not as commonly reported in modern NDEs as it was during the spiritualist movement of the nineteenth century,[29] but modern examples have been noted by near-death researcher Elisabeth Kubler-Ross and others.[30] Morse recorded one NDEr as saying, "I left my body, although I still felt like I was connected to it by a string."[31] In Shirley MacLaine's popular book *Out on a Limb* (1983), she describes an OBE journey— not part of an NDE—during which she noticed that "attached to my spirit was a thin, thin, silver cord that remained stretched though attached to my body."[32] This phenomenon is often interpreted to mean that once the cord is severed, returning to the body is impossible. There may be an intimation of this in the book of Ecclesiastes:

> Remember him—before the silver cord is
>   severed,
>   or the golden bowl is broken;
> before the pitcher is shattered at the spring,
>   or the wheel broken at the well,
> and the dust returns to the ground it came from,
>   and the spirit returns to God who gave it
>   (Ecclesiastes 12:6,7).[33]

The distinction between near-death and biological death led Roman Catholic theologian Hans Küng to make the important point that NDEs reveal something about the process of dying but nothing about death itself. For him, NDEs imply nothing about an eternal life after death. Although dying is the way to the final destination of the soul, no NDEr has reached that destination.[34] Küng is right to emphasize the difference between "eternal life" and the limitations of the NDE. However, if the OBE aspect of at least some NDEs can be established (as argued in chapter 4), then the NDE does give good evidence for the existence of the soul and its separability from the body—which makes the eternal existence of the soul after biological death easier to accept.[35]

THE TIBETAN DEAD

In the popular book *The Tibetan Book of Living and Dying* (1992)—which is based on *The Tibetan Book of the Dead*—Sogyal Rinpoche observes that whatever NDEs mean, they do not represent the final stage of death. In describing the similarities and differences between modern NDEs and death according to the Tibetan Buddhist tradition, Rinpoche writes:

> The greatest difference, of course, is the fact that the near-death experiencers do *not* die, whereas the [Tibetan Buddhist] teachings describe what happens to people as they die, after actual physical death, and as they take rebirth. The fact that the near-death experiencers do not go further on the journey into death—some are only "dead" for one minute—must go some way to explaining the possibility for disparities between the two accounts.[36]

Although Moody mentions *The Tibetan Book of the Dead* as a source that correlates with his findings, he grants that it "includes many later stages of death which none of my subjects have gone so far as to experience."[37] Moody fails to mention that, for Tibetan Buddhism, the final state of death is the dissolving of the individual self prior to reincarnation.[38] This dissolution of the self is not experienced by NDErs. (It would, after all, be impossible to experience.) Nor would the idea of it appeal to someone who would rather live eternally "in the light" as an individual than cease to exist as an individual and be reincarnated as another person.[39]

Moreover, according to Tibetan Buddhism, states after death but before dissolution are regarded as merely projections of the individual's mind. They are not viewed as concrete, objective realities. Rinpoche says, "Once we mistake the appearances [of NDEs] as separate from us, as 'external visions,' we respond with fear or hope, which leads us into delusion."[40] The editor of an earlier edition of the *Tibetan Book of the Dead* commented that the pre-dissolution visions "are not visions of reality, but nothing more than (one's own) intellectual impulses which have assumed personified form."[41] This is quite at odds with the typical understanding of NDEs as conveying some truth about an actual, objective spiritual reality after death.

DID BETTY EADIE REALLY DIE?

The more influential the NDE account, the more important is the question of whether clinical death can be verified. *Embraced by the Light* enjoys immense popularity largely because Betty Eadie claims to have received spiritual insights from Jesus Christ and other angelic beings in the heavenly realm while she was dead. For this claim to be true, Eadie must at least have been clinically dead. Several important elements of her story, however, suggest that she may not have been clinically dead at the time of her experience.

Eadie waited almost 20 years to publish her alleged 1973 NDE. Why so long a wait? NDE researchers prefer to deal with accounts as quickly as possible after clinical death so as to be assured of a more accurate record of what occurred.[42]

Another question is why Eadie, thus far,[43] has refused to release her medical records, to name the hospital where she stayed, or even to name the doctor who was in charge during the time she had her experience.[44] Eadie has said that her doctor is now deceased.[45] She has also stated, "The exact length of time I was dead and whatnot were not documented, so I don't have those facts,"[46] and "I can't prove it happened. But I know it's true."[47] When asked by the *Christian Research Journal* if she intended to release her medical records, she replied, "No, I doubt it."[48] She explains this refusal by saying, "I don't need credibility. I'm not trying to prove my experience, I'm sharing it."[49]

From the few details Eadie *has* supplied, it is possible to piece the following together. She had a partial hysterectomy in the morning and regained consciousness in the afternoon, when her doctor told her the surgery had been successful and that she would be feeling fine shortly. After falling asleep for a time, she awoke and rang for a nurse to get her some water. The nurse said that her husband and some friends had visited, but she did not recall it. At 9:00 P.M., a nurse brought Eadie her evening medication. Except for a little pain from the surgery, she felt fine. A half hour later, she felt light-headed and chilled and wanted to sleep; within minutes after this, her alleged NDE began.[50]

Details are also sparse as to events following her supposed return to her body. Immediately after reentering her body, the three spirit "monks" came to comfort her; she then fell asleep until 2:00 A.M. She did not know how long she had been "in the spirit world," or whether anyone had been in her room or if anything had been done to revive her. There appeared to be no evidence that any medical intervention had taken place.

Eadie then experienced a terrifying demonic encounter, and the "monks" returned to rescue and encourage her. She telephoned her husband, who came immediately. Eadie remembers that around this time, anxious doctors and nurses were working on her. She doesn't know what they were doing or how long they had been there, but she says that for the next few hours they came in and out of her room to check on her.[51]

Five years after Eadie's "death," she plucked up some courage and went to talk to her doctor about what had happened that night. The doctor, Eadie claims, told her that she had hemorrhaged during the surgery, and that there had indeed been complications that night. She reports that "it appeared that the hemorrhage [had] occurred again later that night," and as a result "they *had* lost me for a while but had felt that it was best not to mention anything to me."[52]

Questioning Eadie's Story

Hemorrhage is a term that describes massive bleeding. *The American Heritage Dictionary* defines the noun *hemorrhage* as an "excessive discharge of blood from the blood vessels; profuse bleeding." It defines the verb "to bleed copiously."[53] Since this is the term Eadie supposedly got from her doctor, and since a doctor should know how to use the term correctly, we can assume that she had massive bleeding during her surgery.

If so, Eadie would most likely have been hooked up to a blood drip after surgery, either in her room or in the ICU.[54] The complications entailed by this procedure contradict the sparse details Eadie gives us. Unless Eadie had been a victim of gross medical neglect, her family, the nurses, and Eadie herself would have been notified that her postsurgical condition was serious. Furthermore, family members would probably have stayed by her throughout the day and evening, and the nursing staff would have been checking her at least every half hour for the first few hours following the surgery. None of this squares with Eadie's statement that the doctor had told her the operation had been "a success." Nor is it consistent with the sense of normality Eadie conveys when describing the time spent alone in her room after the surgery and prior to the NDE.

There are other apparent inconsistencies. Eadie claims to have died and undergone her NDE shortly after 9:30 P.M. To set the stage for this, she gives her readers the sense that she was pretty much left alone by the nursing staff because she was recovering nicely; that is, she wasn't being checked on every 15 or 30 minutes. After taking her medication at 9:00 P.M. she was left to fall asleep for the night. In this context, she suddenly dies, with no one likely to come in to check on her right away. This is important because, as noted earlier, a patient normally cannot remain clinically dead for more than six minutes without becoming biologically dead. Let's say that Eadie went the distance and remained "dead" for six minutes. If there were no doctors or nurses in her room at the time to administer CPR, why didn't she pass on to biological death after six minutes? Even if, for the sake of argument, we extend the time of her clinical death to 10 or 15 minutes, we still have to ask the same tough question.

Had medical personnel entered her room and resuscitated Eadie shortly after her "death" at 9:30 P.M.? Eadie says, "Nobody was aware that I had died."[55] Her supposedly lifeless body lay alone in the room. She evidently does not know what time it was when she "slipped back" into her body, but she does describe her room as looking just as it had when she "left" it. There was no one in the room, and no indication that anyone had been in the room to resuscitate her. She fell asleep after returning to her body; she doesn't know for how long. When she awoke it was 2:00 A.M.[56]

At this time, her room was still empty, although it soon became populated with assorted spirit beings. The first human to enter her room was her husband, arriving in response to her phone call. Only after her husband showed up did Eadie become aware of doctors and nurses attending to her, which they

evidently were doing with some urgency.[57] This *does* sound
like emergency medical treatment, but it did not occur until
after 2:00 A.M.—over four-and-a-half hours after whatever
supposedly triggered her NDE. Eadie reports that she "continued to view the spirit world during this time,"[58] and this may
have included elements of a genuine NDE. But she does not tell
us of these experiences.

The four-and-a-half-hour gap between the time Eadie claims
to have had her NDE and the time she apparently received
emergency medical treatment makes her story doubtful. If
Eadie re-hemorrhaged and, as a result, entered clinical death
around 9:30 P.M., and if no medical personnel tended to her
until after 2:00 A.M., then her body would have had to recover
of its own accord not only from the hemorrhage and it effects,
but also from clinical death (cessation of breathing and heartbeat). This, medically speaking, is highly improbable. It is
more probable that, if Eadie had hemorrhaged and died and not
been resuscitated, she would have been biologically dead by
the time the doctors and nurses came into her room four-and-
a-half hours later.

In conclusion, it appears likely that either Eadie was not
clinically dead at the time of her "NDE," or she was biologically dead. Since the latter could not be the case—barring a
miracle of biblical proportions, for which we have no evidence—
we are left with serious questions as to whether Eadie's experience of being "embraced by the light" could have had anything
at all to do with life after death. If Eadie did not clinically die
and have some kind of NDE on the evening of her surgery, the
only options for explaining the experience she recounts are
that it is a fabrication, a vivid dream, a hallucination, an out-
of-the-body experience, a spiritual deception, or some combination of these factors.

Given the amazing popularity of Eadie's book and the gulli-
bility of many people—not to mention the dire eternal consequences of believing her message if it is untrue—it seems
unwarranted for Eadie to expect us simply to take her word for
it. But, of course, even if she were to verify her clinical death,
that in itself would not prove that the *message* of her NDE is
true, as we have argued throughout this book.[59]

In pursuing the significance of the NDE, we next will con-
sult the Bible. Does it give instances of NDEs, as many claim?
Do its teachings agree or disagree with the reports given by
NDErs?

8

THE BIBLE AND THE
NEAR-DEATH
EXPERIENCE

Every word of God is flawless; he is a shield to those
who take refuge in him.

—Proverbs 30:5

It would be unwise to build a philosophy of life, death, and the afterlife on NDE reports, given their penultimate nature and their often contradictory spiritual messages. Researchers themselves are aware of this. Kenneth Ring acknowledges that "what may happen after the initial stages of death—something this [NDE] research cannot speak to—remains an open question."[1] When a hot-air balloon climbs into the sky, the air is pure, the sky is blue, and all is well. However, it would be foolish to assume that such initial conditions of ascent are likely to continue all the way to the atmosphere of the moon. Despite his own elaborate NDE, George Ritchie writes, "I have no idea what the next life will be like. Whatever I saw was only—from the doorway, so to speak. But it was enough to convince me . . . that consciousness does not cease with physical death."[2]

The issue of discrepant NDEs also suggests the possibility of spiritual misperception or even deception. Consider two NDEs mentioned in chapter 6. In one, a spirit told a woman that there is no sin. In another, a practicing homosexual was told by a being he took to be Jesus Christ that he should forsake his homosexual behavior and honor the heavenly Father. The second account presupposes sin as a reality to be renounced, while the first denies its reality entirely. Simply put, both of these accounts cannot express the same spiritual reality, because their messages are contradictory. It cannot be true that there is sin and that there is no sin. That would be nonsense.

NEAR-DEATH ERROR

In order to avoid nonsense and pursue truth, we need to dispense with the assumption that NDErs are free from significant spiritual deception. Although some researchers insist that all positive NDEs are of the same reality but are simply described differently, the fact is that many accounts of NDEs differ so significantly that they could not all be referring to the same truth.

A fascinating account by Maurice Rawlings highlights what is at stake. Rawlings interviewed a rough-looking 21-year-old man who wanted to donate plasma. When Rawlings questioned the man about several recent wounds that might infect others, the man reluctantly confessed to having killed two people. He also had been shot by a transvestite after beating him up for deceiving him into thinking he was a woman. While receiving CPR in an ambulance, this man had undergone an NDE that included passing through a tunnel and seeing a heavenly, welcoming light. When Rawlings asked him how he felt about that, the man said:

> Well, it felt good to be in this beautiful place, you know, but I kept wondering why the light never asked me about my beating the heck out of the cross-

dresser. And the light never mentioned the two kill-ings in the past.

I was glad he didn't ask me about those things, but if he was from God, why didn't he? I thought about bringing it up, but said to myself, "Why knock a good thing?" and kept my mouth shut. I knew I should be in hell instead of this nice place, but I kept quiet.[3]

Perplexed, the man then asked Rawlings, "Doc, does God ever make mistakes?"[4] This confused fellow seemed to have a better moral sense and theology than the being of light itself.[5] Few people would claim that God, the all-perfect being, makes mistakes or is forgetful. This man wisely questioned the mean-ing of his experience. By way of contrast, Dannion Brinkley said that early on in his NDE, "I put my trust in the Being of Light."[6] Was this wise? Should we trust what we hear carte blanche?

The question is one of discernment. We have argued that some NDEs are real; that is, they cannot be dismissed as mere illusions of a dying brain.[7] However, the deeper question is not of its reality but of its identity. If the NDE is not "just in the mind" but is an experience of objective reality, then it is pos-sible that a mask is being worn. A cross-dresser is a real person, but one with a deceptive facade that misidentifies who he is. Similarly, a spiritual experience may be real and yet false. Phillip Swihart explains:

Even if we could demonstrate that the near-death experiences occurred during death, we would have to evaluate the character of those experiences and determine whether they provide insight into the way things really are.[8]

To try to identify its meaning and message, many NDE enthusiasts, such as Kenneth Ring, have adopted New Age and other non-Christian perspectives. Others, like Raymond Moody and Betty Eadie, have attempted to draw strong connections between the NDE and the Christian tradition, perhaps because the majority of Americans are theists who have some affinity with Christianity. But we need to question whether or how these connections should be drawn.

ARE NEAR-DEATH EXPERIENCES IN THE BIBLE?

Moody and others claim that the Bible reveals NDEs or phenomena like them. Moody rightly notes that the Bible "is the most widely read and discussed book dealing with matters relating to the nature of the spiritual aspect of man and to life after death."[9] It is therefore appropriate to consider what it may have to say about the NDE.

Paul's Vision of Jesus. Moody finds a parallel to an NDE in the vision of Jesus given to Rabbi Saul of Tarsus, which converted him from a persecutor of Christians to the apostle Paul, a disciple of Jesus Christ. In Acts 26:12-27, Paul tells King Agrippa that on a trip to Damascus years earlier, he saw a blazing light, brighter than the sun, which engulfed him and his companions and forced them to fall to the ground. Then a voice said, "Saul, Saul, why do you persecute me?" Paul asked, "Who are you, Lord?" "I am Jesus, whom you are persecuting," came the reply. Jesus then said,

> I am sending you to them [both Jews and Gentiles] to open their eyes and turn them from darkness to light, and from the power of Satan to God, so that they may receive forgiveness of sins and a place

among those who are sanctified by faith in me (Acts 26:17,18).

Paul was temporarily blinded by the light, but his sight was restored a few days later when a disciple named Ananias prayed for him (Acts 9:10-19).

Moody noted that Paul's experience was similar to an NDE in that it included a vision of a communicating light, it changed Paul's life, and one man declared Paul to be insane (Acts 26:24), just as NDErs sometimes are labeled.[10] Moody also noted that Paul's vision was unlike an NDE in two ways: It did not occur at a point near death, and Paul was physically blinded instead of merely being dazzled by the light.[11] But the vision of Jesus that turned Saul, the enemy of Christians, into Paul, the apostle of Christ, differs from most NDEs in many other respects as well. There was no OBE, no tunnel, no vision of deceased people (besides the resurrected Jesus), no life-review, or any other major NDE elements.

Moody seems to ignore the meaning of Jesus' words to Saul, even though these words disclose a message entirely different from that of the most commonly reported NDEs. Moody's model of the NDE—which downplays or ignores the negative experiences—contradicts Jesus' message to Saul. This comes into sharp relief when we contrast the words of Saul's "being of light" with four impressions that many NDErs receive from their being of light or from the NDE in general.

1. A typical NDE impression is that we should not fear death because we've done nothing in this life to warrant fearing the afterlife.

Although Jesus does not specifically mention death, he implies that it can only be welcomed without fear if one has turned "from the power of Satan to God" in order to receive "forgiveness of sins" through "faith in me" (Acts 26:18).

Without the forgiveness of sins and deliverance from the power of Satan, one cannot be without fear of a morally perfect God and the eternal consequences of unforgiven sin.

2. Another common NDE message is that there is no judgment. The being of light accepts everyone and rejects no one. There is no hell.

However, if God's policy were to accept all people regardless of their moral state or spiritual orientation, it would have been absurd for Jesus to have instructed Paul to "open their eyes" to the spiritual realities vital to their finding "a place among those who are sanctified by faith" in Jesus (verse 18). The word *sanctified* is not commonly used today. In the Bible it means "set apart" to a holy God or "distinguished" from sin.

Evidently, Jesus was explaining to Saul that as people receive forgiveness and experience the power of God by faith, they will be morally transformed. This sets them apart for God's purposes and distinguishes them from those who have not yet entered into the experience of divine forgiveness, power, and love.

As was mentioned in chapter 5, Jesus spoke frequently of hell as a literal place of everlasting alienation from God, reserved for those who refuse forgiveness on God's terms and so remain enslaved to Satan's power. Yet Betty Eadie and many other NDErs claim that no one will go to hell.[12]

3. The NDEs commonly reported by Moody, Ring, Morse, and others neglect any mention of Jesus Christ as the unique agent of spiritual liberation (what the Bible calls "salvation"). Instead, people are considered to be already "one with God." The being of light may be identified as Jesus in some cases, but this Jesus does not usually seem to be the Jesus of the New Testament. For example, Moody reported an NDEr who said that "the light was Christ—a consciousness, a oneness with all

things."[13] This does not harmonize with the words Jesus spoke to Saul.

First, Saul is not "one" with Jesus in the sense of sharing Jesus' divine identity, or he would not have cowered before the majesty of the resurrected and radiant Jesus (see also Revelation 1:12-18). Second, Jesus teaches about the existence of good and evil, not about a divine oneness of all things. He speaks of people turning from the power of Satan (evil) to the power of God (good) (Acts 26:18). Third, Jesus distinguishes those who are set apart by faith in him from those who are not. The Jesus of Saul's vision knows nothing of pantheistic monism.[14]

4. In NDEs there is often the sense that religious doctrines don't matter; one should simply gain knowledge and become more loving.

The goals of becoming more loving and knowledgeable are not contradicted by Jesus' revelation to Saul. Yet Jesus' message contained no vague generalities. When Paul defended himself before King Agrippa, he declared, "I am saying nothing beyond what the prophets and Moses said would happen—that the Christ would suffer and, as the first to rise from the dead, would proclaim light to his own people and to the Gentiles" (Acts 26:22,23).

Paul's encounter with the light that was Jesus compelled him to proclaim that light to everyone he could reach, no matter what the cost. In fact, Paul was being tried by King Agrippa because of his declaration of Jesus' message. Generalities about divine love and a no-questions-asked acceptance of generic spirituality would have stirred up little trouble with the governing authorities and would have left no mark on world history. Unlike many NDErs, Paul did not have a universalistic or syncretistic view of religions as being one in essence. For Paul, Jesus was the prime reality one must know, and his truth excluded all error.

The Spiritual Body. Moody appeals to Paul's statements about the "spiritual body" in 1 Corinthians 15:35-44, which he correlates with NDErs' reports of leaving their physical bodies. Moody believes the NDE's emphasis on the disembodied soul harmonizes with Paul's view here.[15]

Paul does speak of Christians leaving their bodies at death to be with their Lord (2 Corinthians 5:1-5; Philippians 1:23,24). But in 1 Corinthians 15, he is describing the Christian's resurrected body, which will be raised by God at the end of history. The reference is to life after death in a new body, not life without a body.

The phrase "spiritual body" means a resurrected body perfectly animated by the Holy Spirit and free from the power of sin and corruption.

> "Spiritual body" does not mean a nonmaterial body, but . . . a physical one similar to the present natural body organizationally, but radically different in that it will be imperishable, glorious and powerful, fit to live eternally with God. There is continuity, but there is also change.[16]

The spiritual body to which Paul refers is still in the future; it will come forth at the resurrection of the dead at the end of history as we know it. This has nothing to do with what NDErs experience. Again, Moody hasn't done his homework.

The Vision of Stephen. Moody also alludes to Stephen's martyrdom (wrongly referring to him as an "apostle") as "a possible near-death experience."[17] Acts chapter 7 tells us that while Stephen was preaching a message to his fellow Jews to accept Jesus as the Messiah, they became furious with him. "But Stephen, full of the Holy Spirit, looked up to heaven and saw the glory of God, and Jesus standing at the right hand of

God. 'Look,' he said, 'I see heaven open and the Son of Man standing at the right hand of God' " (Acts 7:55,56). After this, the irate crowd screamed at him, dragged him out of town, and began to stone him. During the stoning, Stephen said, "Lord Jesus, receive my spirit," and "Lord, do not hold this sin against them" (Acts 7:59,60). Then he died.

Nothing is recorded about Stephen's experience after he died. This is not "a possible near-death experience"; it is the experience of someone who was in good health up until the time he was executed. Stephen's vision of God the Father and Jesus Christ occurred while he was fully alive; it was not a near-death vision of a generic being of light. In fact, no light is mentioned. Stephen's theology is also at odds with much of what comes from commonly reported NDEs. He asks Jesus to forgive his executioners' sin of breaking God's commandment not to murder (Exodus 20:13). Stephen's statement presupposes that God is a personal and morally impeccable being who has been sinned against by his creatures—creatures who desperately need forgiveness through the Jesus to whom Stephen prayed.

Paul Out of the Body? Another way people use the Bible to try to substantiate the NDE is by referring to Paul's rather cryptic account of being "caught up" to heaven:

> I know a person in Christ who fourteen years ago was caught up to the third heaven—whether in the body or out of the body I do not know; God knows. And I know that such a person—whether in the body or out of the body I do not know; God knows—was caught up into Paradise and heard things that are not to be told, that no mortal is permitted to repeat (2 Corinthians 12:2-4 NRSV).

Melvin Morse somewhat glibly refers to this statement by the apostle Paul as illustrative of the kinds of NDEs he describes in his book *Closer to the Light*.[18] Yet there is no mention in Paul's account of a rushing sound, a tunnel, deceased people, a great light, a life-review, or any typical NDE elements.

Despite Paul's reticence to explain this matter in more detail, some Christians circulated a phony but influential Greek text during the third century, which claimed to fill in the missing metaphysical details of Paul's experience.[19] But Paul clearly stated that he was not "permitted to repeat" what he had experienced in "the third heaven" or in "Paradise" (words that refer to God's dwelling place). What the apostle does say, however, is untypical of most NDErs' stories.

First, Paul doesn't know if his experience took place in or out of the body. If it were in the body, it would have nothing in common with the NDE, which occurs out of the body. However, by allowing that he might have been out of the body at the time, Paul does grant the possibility of the soul leaving the body to be with God prior to irreversible, biological death.

Second, even if this experience did take place outside of his body, Paul says nothing about being near death at the time. Some have speculated that Paul was recounting a vision he had received when he was left for dead after having been stoned at Lystra (Acts 14:19,20). This is highly speculative, since the Bible only says that the Jews who stoned him *thought* he was dead. They may have been mistaken; we don't know. In *Saved by the Light*, Dannion Brinkley makes the mistake of confusing Paul's stoning at Lystra with his "NDE" on the road to Damascus.[20] When Paul recounts his stoning, he says nothing about dying (2 Corinthians 11:25). Even if he did die and then got revived at Lystra, this doesn't mean he had the vision of paradise at that time.

Third, although Paul goes on to mention the "surpassingly great revelations" (2 Corinthians 12:7) he received during this experience, he does not make them the basis for his ministry or his message about Jesus; for he was not allowed to explain them to anyone. Paul is far more reserved than many of his interpreters.

Fourth, whatever happened to Paul, his experience could not be representative of NDEs in general because he is referring only to "a person *in Christ*" (verse 2), that is, a Christian. We cannot infer from his words that all people who claim to leave the body experience what Paul, "a person in Christ," experienced. The Bible teaches that people who are not "in Christ" at death have a very different ultimate destination from those who are "in Christ."

These biblical investigations challenge Morse's syncretistic speculation that "many of the world's religious leaders have been driven by profound near-death and other visionary experiences that involve the mystical light."[21] Near-death experience certainly did not "drive" Jesus or his disciples. Although Morse attempts to link religious leaders as diverse as Jonathan Edwards (a Calvinist theologian) and Swami Yogananda (a pantheistic Hindu) on the basis of their references to divine light, a study of biblical teaching shows that the light of Jesus Christ cannot be identified with the "light" of any pantheistic, monistic experience.[22]

HOW IMPORTANT IS THE NEAR-DEATH EXPERIENCE?

Because the Bible does not describe any NDEs, we can conclude that it does not view them as crucial for our understanding of life, death, and the beyond. Even when Jesus miraculously raised his friend Lazarus from biological death, the Bible does not record anything about any experience Lazarus had while his body was in the tomb for four days (John 11:1-44).

Although the Bible teaches that the soul separates from the body at death, it does not predict that those who return from clinical death will have an NDE to report. Nor does it assume that any experiences occurring at clinical death should serve as the final word on the afterlife. Therefore, from a biblical perspective, all NDEs could be delusional in one way or another without this affecting the Bible's teaching on the afterlife. If some NDEs are spiritual experiences apart from the body, as I believe some are, this would provide some evidence for an afterlife. But such evidence still leaves many questions unanswered—unless we consult the Bible as our authority. The NDE has only a very limited value as an indicator of postmortem truth.

Near-death experiences often differ too substantially to be reconciled even to each other, let alone to the Bible. Although some NDE researchers and others appeal to the Bible to justify the existence and importance of NDEs, the Bible says little if anything about the NDE. The near-death experience is not crucial to biblical teaching regarding life after death or, for that matter, life before death. What *is* crucial is the resurrection of Jesus Christ and its eternal implications.

JESUS' RESURRECTION AND THE AFTERLIFE

The Christian faith is rooted in one who has returned from the dead, not as an NDEr, but as the risen Lord of the universe. More than anything else, the resurrection of Jesus Christ distinguishes Christianity from other religions. Because no other religion is based on the physical resurrection of its founder, Christianity cannot be synthesized with other faiths. The Christian faith depends on the historical fact of Christ's resurrection from the dead. As the apostle Paul observed, if Christ has not been raised, preaching the gospel is useless, Christian faith is futile, there is no forgiveness of sin, and there is no hope for heaven (1 Corinthians 15:14-19). But, Paul proclaimed, "Christ has indeed been raised from the dead" (15:20). Because of this, Christians believe that they, too, will one day be raised from the dead and given bodies that are imperishable.

> Our citizenship is in heaven. And we eagerly await a Savior from there, the Lord Jesus Christ, who, by the power that enables him to bring everything under his control, will transform our lowly bodies so that they will be like his glorious body (Philippians 3:20,21).

This resurrection hope is not a leap of faith in the dark. Many factors make belief in Christ's resurrection credible and attractive to those thirsting for endless life. First, testimony to his resurrection came quickly after his crucifixion and was made by eyewitnesses and by people who had consulted eyewitnesses (Luke 1:1-4; 2 Peter 1:16). There was no time for a legend to develop and a resurrection myth to be added to the story of Jesus and his followers. Here is what the apostle Paul had to say:

> I handed on to you as of first importance what I in turn had received: that Christ died for our sins in accordance with the scriptures, and that he was buried, and that he was raised on the third day in accordance with the scriptures, and that he appeared to Cephas, then to the twelve. Then he appeared to more than five hundred brothers and sisters at one time, most of whom are still alive, though some have died. Then he appeared to James, then to all the apostles. Last of all . . . he appeared also to me (1 Corinthians 15:3-8 NRSV).

Paul wrote this some time in the mid-50s, and throughout it he quotes from well-known sayings that were circulating very soon after Jesus' death. This shows that the newborn church had a firm conviction that Jesus was no longer dead. All the New Testament books, which were written by people who were in a good position to report accurately the events they recorded, affirm the resurrection of Christ as a historical fact that was central to the gospel.[23]

Second, it is impossible to explain adequately the origin and growth of Christianity without Jesus' resurrection. Virtually all scholars of New Testament history agree that Jesus died by crucifixion, that his original disciples were thrown into despair, that they came to believe that he was raised from the dead, that this transformed them from despair to courageous hope followed by proclamation, and that Paul was converted to Christianity through an extraordinary vision which was thought to be of the resurrected Christ. The actual physical resurrection of Jesus Christ from the dead is the best explanation for these historical facts.[24]

Since the apostles preached the resurrected Jesus in the vicinity where he had been crucified, their gospel could have been refuted decisively simply by exhuming and exposing the corpse of Jesus. Both the Roman government and the Jewish religious leaders would have been motivated to refute the young Christians, but they did not because they could not produce the body. He had risen.

Furthermore, if Jesus had remained in a tomb, in all likelihood the tomb would have been venerated, as were at least 50 tombs of religious leaders during that time.[25] But we have only the record of an empty tomb. Even those who opposed the Christian movement granted the fact of Jesus' empty tomb (Matthew 28:11-15).

If Jesus had not been raised, it would be difficult to explain why the early church instituted two religious practices—

baptism and the Lord's supper—that presuppose Jesus' resurrection. Christian baptism was perpetuated on the basis of the analogy that just as Christ died and was resurrected, so the Christian dies to a life of sin and is raised by Christ to a new life (Romans 6:1-14). The Lord's supper (or communion) is not simply a memorial meal, but a *celebration* that Jesus Christ was both sacrificed and raised from the dead. When Paul says that this practice "proclaim[s] the Lord's death *until he comes*" (1 Corinthians 11:26, my emphasis), he assumes that Jesus is no longer dead but alive as the resurrected Lord who will come again. Baptism and the Lord's supper would be meaningless apart from the literal resurrection of Christ.[26]

Moreover, why would the early Jewish converts to Christianity have shifted the day of worship from Saturday (the day God originally ordained) to resurrection Sunday (Acts 20:7), had not Easter morning altered their understanding? Jewish believers did not play fast and loose with a central teaching of the Old Testament. Christ's resurrection is the best explanation for their new day of worship.

Third, the alternative theories given to refute the resurrection fall short. The disciples could not have been deceivers preaching a resurrection they knew to be a hoax, simply because there was no reason for them to do so. Why be persecuted for what you know to be a lie? Blaise Pascal summarizes the matter cogently:

> The hypothesis that the Apostles were knaves is quite absurd. Follow it to the end and imagine these twelve men meeting after Jesus' death and conspiring to say that he had risen from the dead. This means attacking all the powers that be. The human heart is singularly susceptible to fickleness, to change, to promises, to bribery. One of them had only to deny his story under these inducements, or still more

because of possible imprisonment, tortures, and death, and they would all have been lost. Follow that out.[27]

The disciples could not have been deceived themselves because Jesus appeared to many of them at different times and in different places in order to leave no room for doubt. The idea that *all* of these appearances were hallucinations or some other kind of deception is just too implausible.

Some people claim that the accounts of Jesus' resurrection were simply invented by later myth-making writers. But this ignores the character of the New Testament documents themselves, which do not read like myths but as datable history (see Luke 1:1-4).[28]

THE SIGNIFICANCE OF JESUS' RESURRECTION

Jesus' resurrection is not merely an oddity that happens to inspire some religious people. On the contrary, this unmatched event uniquely demonstrates Jesus' supreme authority over every power, including that of death itself. He predicted his own crucifixion and resurrection (Matthew 16:21), and after his resurrection Jesus told his disciples, "All authority in heaven and on earth has been given to me" (Matthew 28:18). Paul affirmed that Jesus "was declared with power to be the Son of God by his resurrection" (Romans 1:4).

Jesus spoke as the one who had mastered death and who offers life to all who come to him. When the resurrected and glorified Jesus appeared to John, he said, "I am the First and the Last. I am the Living One; I was dead, and behold I am alive for ever and ever. And I hold the keys of death and Hades" (Revelation 1:17,18). Because Jesus himself died and was raised from the dead never to die again, he has authority over death.

Jesus shared our humanity "so that by his death he might destroy him who holds the power of death—that is, the devil—and free those who all their lives were held in slavery by their fear of death" (Hebrews 2:14,15; see also Romans 6:9,10; Hebrews 7:24,25). C.S. Lewis draws out the implications:

> The New Testament writers speak as if Christ's achievement in rising from the dead was the first event of its kind in the whole history of the universe. He is the "first fruits," the "pioneer of life." He has forced open a door that has been locked since the death of the first man. He has met, fought, and beaten the King of Death. Everything is different because He has done so. This is the beginning of the New Creation: a new chapter in cosmic history has opened.[29]

Unlike the NDEr, Jesus did not merely visit near-death, only to be spared through resuscitation. He died as no other ever has died. He died as a sacrifice, paying the penalty for the sins of sinful people, in order that those who accept his sacrifice through repentance might have the perfect righteousness of Christ imputed to them (Isaiah 53; 2 Corinthians 5:21; Galatians 3–4, Romans 3–5).[30]

Jesus' corpse was not jump-started; it was transformed by God into a new level of incorruptible existence. He returned from biological death through the miracle-working power of God. Jesus' resurrected body is not mortal like ours, but neither is it purely spiritual or an entirely new entity (Luke 24:39,40). Jesus came back as a butterfly from the cocoon of death. NDErs come back as star-struck caterpillars.

Jesus Christ's resurrection gives his followers the certainty that they, too, will be with him after death (Philippians 1:23,24; 2 Corinthians 5:1-8), and that their bodies will be raised from the dead at the end of the age (1 Corinthians 15:20-23). It is from the unparalleled and utterly reliable word of the risen Christ that we truly understand the meaning of life, death, and the afterlife, and not from the incomplete and often contradictory testimonies of the near-dead.

Yet many NDErs claim that, as a result of their experience, they have tapped into the same power to which Jesus himself had access. We now turn to these claims of psychic empowerment.

9

PSYCHIC POWERS

Do not believe every spirit, but test the spirits to see whether they are from God, because many false prophets have gone out into the world.

—The apostle John (1 John 4:1)

It is often thought that psychic powers accompany or follow a near-death experience because a taste of the afterlife awakens a dormant psychic reservoir in the near-death experiencer. For many, this aspect of the NDE guarantees that the experience is genuine and good. In order to assess this claim, we need to consider what NDErs report about enhanced psychic abilities and then evaluate what these reports indicate about the nature of the NDE.

The term *psychic* can refer to many things, but I will use it to designate experiences that cannot be explained through the normal laws of nature or the operation of the physical senses. A genuinely psychic experience brings a supernatural dimension into play to produce extraordinary results. Examples include out-of-the-body experiences (OBEs), extrasensory perception (ESP), telepathy, precognition (knowing the future), spirit visitation, and contacting the dead or other disembodied spirits through mediumship or channeling. With the advent of the New Age movement, increasing numbers of people are becoming fascinated by and involved in the psychic realm.[1]

PSYCHIC POWERS AND THE
NEAR-DEATH EXPERIENCE

The psychic dimension may be experienced during or after an NDE, or both. One prominent case is that of Dannion Brinkley, who records his two NDEs in his bestselling book *Saved by the Light*. Brinkley claims to have found himself in a strange world after having been electrocuted by a lightning strike that was carried through the telephone lines to the telephone on which he was speaking. He left his body, encountered a being of light, had a life-review, and later was addressed by a council of 13 beings (one more than Eadie's council of 12 men) who, he claims, foretold the future by opening videocassette-sized boxes that displayed upcoming events.[2]

Brinkley states that most of the spirit council's predictions—including the fall of the Soviet Union and the Gulf War—have come true, while several others are pending. He says that of 117 events foretold during his NDE, 95 have taken place.[3] In Raymond Moody's foreword to the book, he claims that Brinkley recounted several of these predictions to him before they occurred.[4]

Brinkley claims that through his NDE he received the ability to read minds, which he discovered by answering people's questions before they finished asking them. He says that once he almost wrecked a business deal by reading the minds of the Norwegian businessmen with whom he was negotiating, despite the fact that he doesn't know Norwegian. He also claims to have profited from his new power through gambling, which he later renounced in order to focus on more benevolent uses of his psychic abilities.[5] Reflecting on these abilities, Brinkley says,

> If there is any consolation in having psychic abilities, it is that other near-death experiencers have

them, too. I don't mean just the experience itself, which is an intense psychic event. I mean what happens after the experience. I have yet to meet a person who has had a near-death experience who does not have flashes of precognition or very well-developed intuitive powers. It makes sense, since people who have had a near-death experience have had nature broken down for them into the very essence of life.[6]

Do these supposedly psychic abilities result from NDEs because people gain insight into "the very essence of life," or are there other explanations for these phenomena?

Melvin Morse believes that these powers are given through the experience of the light, because the light activates the dormant parts of the brain that are responsible for psychic powers.[7] He even theorizes that the NDE changes the electromagnetic field of NDErs, since NDErs seem to produce strange phenomena in connection with electrical devices. Morse claims that one-fourth of the NDErs he has studied cannot consistently wear watches because they repeatedly break down.[8] P.M.H. Atwater, an NDEr and author, makes the same claim about herself.[9]

However, meticulous research is required in order to verify these events and powers as legitimately "psychic." When Morse speaks of verifying psychic claims, he doesn't specify how this could be done consistently.[10] Some claims of psychic power may only involve successful guesswork or even self-deception. Considering Brinkley's claim, it is convenient for him to have published his predictions about the fall of the USSR and the Gulf War after they occurred. Painstaking research on famous psychics such as Uri Geller and James Hydrick has exposed them as clever tricksters who created the illusion of psychic phenomena.[11] Of course, not all who falsely claim

these powers are deceivers; some may simply be deceived into
thinking they possess powers they do not have.

But even if some NDErs do experience a significant increase
in psychic powers, what does this prove? Does it authenticate
the NDEs' messages about spiritual reality?

PSYCHIC POWERS FOR
A NEW AGE?

Some writers see NDErs' psychic abilities and increased
spiritual awareness as important signs that the collective consciousness of the planet is rising, that a New Age of greater
harmony and spiritual maturity may be dawning. Kenneth
Ring, taking a cue from New Age theorist Teilhard de Chardin,
calls this "Omega." Ring believes that the NDE is simply one
type of mystical occurrence that mystics and seers have been
experiencing for millennia, and which now is serving as a kind
of cosmic evolutionary trigger into a global higher consciousness. In his book *The Omega Project* (1992), Ring speaks of the
transformative power of NDEs, as well as close encounters
with UFOs, as manifestations of what he calls "Mind at Large."
By this term—borrowed from English novelist, philosopher,
and mystic Aldous Huxley—Ring means "a kind of planetary
or collective mind that is both an expression of humanity's
deepest yearnings and transcendent to them."[12]

Ring understands "Mind at Large" in a pantheistic sense;
that is, the inner divinity of the planet and the human condition
is manifesting itself through non-ordinary states of consciousness, including the psychic realm. In his first book, *Life at
Death*, Ring claims that the light in the NDE is actually one's
"total self" or "higher self"—a reality deeper than the or-
dinary consciousness we have of ourselves as limited and separated beings.[13] "If one can accept the idea of a higher self,"
Ring writes, "it is not difficult to assume that that self...is

actually an aspect of God."[14] Ring also commends a statement from the ancient Greek philosopher Heraclitus that the human soul is infinite.[15]

Although Ring doesn't use the terms, his concepts mirror the theology of nondualistic Hinduism (and many occult beliefs),[16] in which the individual self (Atman) is really one with the higher self (Brahman), or God. This oneness can be experienced through mystical illumination or enlightenment.[17] Through occurrences such as the NDE, Ring believes that "we are experiencing the first bursts of a new self-renewing power for the healing of the earth, with millennial energies that have been liberated through direct contact with the transcendental order."[18]

To account for the psychic powers often imparted by the NDE, Ring likens the NDE to the occult phenomena that historically have been associated with shamans (indigenous folk healers, sorcerers, and mystics). The NDEr "has been inadvertently initiated into the first stages of the shaman's journey."[19] This journey involves entering an altered state of consciousness in which the shaman tries to control and harmonize with various spirit beings for the good of himself and his or her tribe.[20]

Ring further likens NDE psychic effects to the awakening of kundalini energy, which in Hindu thought is believed to be a divine energy coiling at the base of the spine, and which is depicted as a serpent.[21] Kundalini energy is typically associated with the practice of yoga. Ring claims that it is being activated when one experiences ecstatic sensations, severe headaches, tickling or itching under the skin, awareness of internal lights and colors, feelings of hot or cold throughout the body, or bodily tremors for no apparent reason.[22] Ring argues that those having NDEs and UFO encounters are likely to experience these symptoms.[23]

The correlation of kundalini (serpent) energy with the NDE
should give us pause. Although NDE researcher Bruce Greyson says that the concept of kundalini "bears some resem-
blances to the more familiar Holy Spirit,"[24] the supposedly
"divine serpent" is *not* similar to the Holy Spirit. The Holy
Spirit draws people out of their self-centered concerns in order
to recognize and worship the resurrected Jesus Christ; the
focus is not on a serpent power within the self. If one is filled
with the Holy Spirit, it is not because some occult power has
been cultivated; it is because one has received a gift from beyond
oneself (Luke 11:13). Biblically, the serpent is often used to
symbolize the demonic (Genesis 3:1; Revelation 12:9; 20:2).

PSYCHIC DANGERS

The psychic powers that sometimes follow an NDE are not
always beneficial. One woman, Anne, who developed precognition after her NDE, dreamed of her neighbor's dog being run
over the day before it was killed. Another time, she felt that
someone had been injured in a car accident across town, which
she was able to verify. These predictions distressed her family,
especially when she dreamed that someone was going to attempt to murder her brother. Her dream was graphic. "She saw
her brother coming to her out of the car, screaming in pain. He
had blood dripping from both hands and an open wound in his
belly."[25] Two weeks later the nightmare became history when
her brother was shot in his hands and stomach by burglars.
This so disturbed Anne that she went to a neurologist who prescribed a medication that caused her to sleep so deeply that it
quelled her predictive dreams. According to Morse, "Anne
says she would rather have the groggy feeling of being constantly medicated than the recurring psychic experiences."[26]

Psychic knowledge in and of itself may not enhance a person's life, romantic assumptions to the contrary. John Ankerberg and John Weldon consulted extensive occult and psychic materials and concluded that involvement in these areas is ultimately hazardous, even as practitioners themselves often warn.[27] Yoga experts alert people to the physical and spiritual dangers of awakening the kundalini energy through yoga; these dangers include insanity, uncontrollable convulsions, and even death. The serpent's bite can be fatal, just as it first was in the garden (Genesis 3).[28]

Bruce Greyson and Barbara Harris, who have had extensive experience with NDErs, believe that the NDE is "unique among [spiritual] doorways in that it opens to people regardless of whether or not they are seeking enlightenment."[29] People who have had almost no spiritual interests may be unexpectedly ushered into a bizarre theater of otherworldly amazement. Greyson and Harris point out that because the NDE "often occurs to people who are not looking or prepared for spiritual growth, it is particularly likely to lead to a spiritual crisis."[30] The crisis often involves sorting out just what happened in the NDE and how it relates to established religious traditions.

But the crux of the matter is, What is the source of the psychic empowerment? Many NDErs believe it is Jesus Christ. Even though her view of Jesus clearly contradicts the biblical record, Betty Eadie is convinced she was embraced by the light of Jesus. Morse strongly asserts that "to tell a patient who has almost died that they did not sit in the lap of Christ even though they vividly described the experience is a form of patient negligence."[31] Greyson and Harris advise counselors of NDErs not to be concerned with the objective reality of the NDE; rather, "you should never press your own beliefs or interpretations of the experience on the NDEr, but let your conversation be guided by the individual's own account and understanding of the experience."[32] Given the prevalence of claims that Jesus Christ has been experienced in the near-death encounter, we must understand who Jesus claimed to be and whether or not he appears in NDEs and bestows psychic powers.

WHO IS JESUS?

Jesus Christ's identity is important to most Americans. In *Who Do Americans Say That I Am?* (1986), respected pollsters George Gallup, Jr., and George O'Connell observe that America's "image of Christ—while a bit murky in spots—is overwhelmingly favorable."[33] Their poll revealed that 70 percent of Americans affirm that Jesus is God and 91 percent believe that Jesus was a historical figure.[34] When pollster George Barna asked for people's reaction to the statement, "Jesus Christ was crucified, died, and rose from the dead and is spiritually alive today," 74 percent strongly agreed and 11 percent agreed somewhat.[35]

Many of the people who profess these beliefs, however, seem to be biblically illiterate about the historical Jesus. Only 42 percent knew that the Sermon on the Mount (Matthew 5–7) was preached by Jesus, and only 46 percent could name the first four books of the New Testament (the Gospels).[36] We have seen evidence of this biblical illiteracy in claims made by Raymond Moody and Dannion Brinkley that the Bible includes accounts of NDEs.[37] Is the Jesus Christ of the New Testament the same as the Jesus of many NDEs? Does the Jesus of the Bible dispense psychic powers?

Jesus is portrayed in the four Gospels as the Son of God who was sent to declare a message of repentance and human transformation. The message itself is called the "gospel," which means "good news." Jesus exhorted people to turn from their self-centered ways (sins) and to seek God's kingdom—God's way of life under God's sovereign rulership. Jesus taught and lived an exalted moral standard and called people to "be perfect, therefore, as your heavenly Father is perfect" (Matthew

5:48). This penetrating message stirred controversy everywhere, and at the same time produced disciples who came to be called Christians several years after Christ's resurrection and ascension into heaven (Acts 11:26).[38]

Although he taught with brilliance and courage, Jesus was no mere teacher. He was a man of action who astounded the crowds not with showmanship or magic tricks, but through the demonstration of God's supernatural power and a deep, loving compassion that reached all who were open to him, even the lowliest in society. When John the Baptist, Jesus' forerunner, asked about Jesus' credentials, he was told:

> The blind receive their sight, the lame walk, the lepers are cleansed, the deaf hear, the dead are raised, and the poor have good news brought to them. And blessed is anyone who takes no offense at me (Matthew 11:5,6 NRSV).

Central to Jesus' teaching was what he said about himself. Both directly and indirectly he claimed not only to be sent by God the Father but to be God in human form. This is why the Jewish religious leaders were so angry with him and often tried to kill him (John 10:22-39). In professing to be one with the Father (John 10:30; 17:22), Jesus was not speaking about his "higher self" (as Kenneth Ring and other pantheists maintain). He was making the exclusive claim of being one in essence with God.

Jesus also taught that God is a personal and holy being, not an impersonal force, energy, or principle, as is claimed by many NDErs. When he instructed his disciples to pray, "Our Father in heaven, hallowed be your name" (Matthew 6:9), he demonstrated that God is to be revered as morally impeccable and free from all human failings. And Jesus taught that he himself perfectly represented the heavenly Father because he alone is the divine and eternal Son (Luke 22:67-71). In one of his more pointed statements, Jesus cut to the theological heart by announcing, "I am the way and the truth and the life. No one comes to the Father except through me" (John 14:6). He identified himself with the Father, explaining that "if you really knew me, you would know my Father as well" (verse 7).

Jesus proclaimed that his mission was "to seek and to save what was lost" (Luke 19:10). When he said that he "did not come to be served, but to serve, and to give his life as a ransom for many" (Matthew 20:28), he meant that he would offer himself as a sacrifice to die for people's sins so that we could have a relationship with God characterized by love, joy, and peace (John 10:10; 20:31). Jesus summarized his mission in these justly famous words:

> For God so loved the world that he gave his one and only Son, that whoever believes in him shall not perish but have eternal life. For God did not send his Son into the world to condemn the world, but to save the world through him. Whoever believes in him is not condemned, but whoever does not believe stands condemned already because he has not believed in the name of God's one and only Son (John 3:16-18).

In his last meal with his disciples before his crucifixion, Jesus explained how God's love would reconcile sinful people to himself. His body would be broken and his blood shed on the cross in order that through his sacrificial death his followers might receive complete forgiveness from God for their wrongdoing (Matthew 26:26-28).

JESUS, THE AFTERLIFE, AND SPIRITUAL POWER

Jesus was very concerned with the afterlife. When arguing

with those who did not believe in it, he protested that the dead would be raised at the end of history (Matthew 22:23-33). He also affirmed that the soul continues to live apart from the body after physical death. When Jesus hung dying on the cross, he told a repentant criminal who had been crucified with him, "Today you will be with me in paradise" (Luke 23:43). Jesus also declared that in the afterlife he would be the final judge over all nations and people:

> The Father . . . has entrusted all judgment to the Son. . . . And he has given him authority to judge because he is the Son of Man. Do not be amazed at this, for a time is coming when all who are in their graves will hear his voice and come out—those who have done good will rise to live, and those who have done evil will rise to be condemned (John 5:22,27-29).

By "those who have done good," Jesus did not mean those people who earn eternal life through good deeds or those who are innately good. That would have contradicted his teaching that we are all sinners and that no one is able to earn eternal life through one's own merit. Rather, he was referring to the good deeds performed by those who believe in him, which serve as evidence of their faith (Matthew 7:16-20; Ephesians 2:10). Eternal life is a gift from a gracious God; but those who receive it are demonstrably changed for the better (John 6:40; 2 Corinthians 4:16; Philippians 2:12,13).

Jesus said that his followers would receive spiritual empowerment in order to glorify God, serve each other, and reach the world with the gospel message (Acts 1:1-8). But this power from the Holy Spirit is not a psychic or occult ability. It is not a latent power released through mystical or shamanic experiences. It is a gift given by a personal God to be used for his holy purposes.[39]

The gift of the Holy Spirit includes what the New Testament calls the "fruit of the Spirit" and the "gifts of the Spirit." The fruit of the Spirit refers to the moral transformation, or sanctification, experienced by those who submit to Christ; it consists of "love, joy, peace, patience, kindness, goodness, faithfulness, gentleness and self-control" (Galatians 5:22,23). The gifts of the Spirit equip Christians for various ministries; they include such abilities as teaching, preaching, healing, wisdom, and administration (see 1 Corinthians 12–14).

The early church renounced the use of psychic powers and the occult. When the gospel was being proclaimed in Ephesus, new believers in Christ confessed their sins of practicing sorcery and publicly burned their expensive occult scrolls (Acts 19:18-20). They could not serve both Jesus Christ and the occult.

TRUTH VERSUS ERROR

Jesus exposed spiritual error, warned of its consequences, and taught his followers to beware of false prophets, who were like wolves in sheep's clothing because they claimed to represent Jesus but failed to obey him. These imposters would be exposed and rejected by Jesus at the last day (Matthew 7:15-23). He further warned of false Christs who would deceive people through "signs and miracles" (Matthew 24:24). For Jesus, spiritual truth was not a do-it-yourself affair. Ambiguous statements about "being loving" and "gaining knowledge" were not on his agenda. He zealously proclaimed objective and particular spiritual truth, and he charged his followers to conserve this truth and to protect it from corruption because the enemy of truth was always active.

Since Jesus lived on earth as the epitome of goodness and spiritual insight in a world gone wrong, he was keenly aware of the sources and consequences of evil that so opposed his character, his message, and his followers. Despite modern attempts to relegate Satan to a mythical status of ancient superstition, Jesus took the reality of the evil one seriously and literally, and spoke more about him than did any other biblical figure.[40]

The demonic was no theoretical or speculative matter for Jesus. He encountered it. He was directly tempted by the devil to abandon his ministry (Matthew 4:1-11; Luke 4:1-13). By holding to the truth of the Scriptures, Jesus overcame the seductive power of the evil one. Jesus declared that Satan "was a murderer from the beginning, not holding to the truth, for there is no truth in him. When he lies, he speaks his native language, for he is a liar and the father of lies" (John 8:44). Satan's spiritual currency is fatal falsehood. Jesus backed up his own words with action by commanding evil spirits (demons or fallen angels under the command of the devil) to go out of people (Matthew 12:22-37; Mark 5:1-20).

Since the devil traffics in error, he seeks to siphon off whatever truth fails to take root in a person's life. For example, in his parable of the sower and the seed, Jesus explained that "when anyone hears the message about the kingdom [of God] and does not understand it, the evil one comes and snatches away what was sown in his heart" (Matthew 13:19). Jesus identified Satan as the author of equivocation, evasion, and confusion.

Jesus also affirmed the possibility of demonic deception by citing the Hebrew Scriptures (see Matthew 5:17,18; Luke 16:31; John 10:35), where God warns his people that even if "a prophet or one who foretells by dreams" proclaims a "miraculous sign or wonder" that comes to pass, that prophet should not be followed if he says, "Let us follow other gods" (Deuteronomy 13:1-4). This warning grants that an apparently supernatural occurrence can nonetheless be a counterfeit of the truth (see also Revelation 16:13,14). For example, even if some of Dannion Brinkley's predictions are verified as having come to pass, this does not legitimize his spiritual message if it opposes the gospel of Christ. The final test is whether or not the "prophet" teaches the truth as it is revealed in God's Word, the Bible.

The spiritual realm is not uniformly benevolent and trustworthy. We must reckon with the devil, who is the enemy of truth. This is why Jesus taught his disciples to pray to the Father, "deliver us from the evil one" (Matthew 6:13). Not all spiritual experiences are safe or dependable. Spiritual deception is far from rare. If we do not discern and reject deceptive claims to the truth, we will become ensnared in error and mistake darkness for light. It is only by knowing and adhering to the truth of God's Word that we, like Jesus, can discern when the demonic is inducing or influencing spiritual experiences.

SPIRITUAL DISCERNMENT

How does all of this help us to understand the psychic empowerment of the NDE and to discern when the demonic is involved? Though the Bible does not specifically speak of NDEs, Jesus' teaching does give us sound direction for evaluating them. For example, Jesus taught that a person can be on good terms with God only by turning away from sin and following the Savior. Yet, as we have noted repeatedly, sin is either not real or no big thing according to many NDEs. The being of light who exhibits unconditional love in a totally nonjudgmental way flies in the face of Jesus' reality. If Jesus Christ were to appear in an NDE, he would not contradict what he taught while on earth, since "Jesus Christ is the same yesterday and today and forever" (Hebrews 13:8; see also 1:12).

Consider the revelation of the resurrected and exalted Jesus Christ in the book of Revelation. Although not an NDE, it reveals the nature of Jesus Christ today and how he can be recognized. The apostle John says that on the Lord's day he was "in the Spirit"—not out of his body—when he heard a "loud voice like a trumpet" (Revelation 1:10), which directed him to write down what he was about to see:

> I turned around to see the voice that was speaking to me. And when I turned I saw seven golden lampstands, and among the lampstands was someone "like a son of man," dressed in a robe reaching down to his feet and with a golden sash around his chest. His head and hair were white like wool, as white as snow, and his eyes were like blazing fire. His feet were like bronze glowing in a furnace, and his voice was like the sound of rushing waters. In his right hand he held seven stars, and out of his mouth came a sharp double-edged sword. His face was like the sun shining in all its brilliance (Revelation 1:12-16).

The reference to "the son of man" is to the Messiah (Jesus) as described by the prophet Daniel (Daniel 7:9-14). In John's vision, Jesus is dressed like the high priest of the Old Testament (Exodus 28:4; 29:5), which depicts his role of providing the sacrifice for our sins and of interceding on our behalf before the throne of God (Hebrews 7:25-27). The white hair signifies maturity, wisdom, and dignity (Leviticus 19:32; Proverbs 16:31). The sword symbolizes divine judgment (Isaiah 49:2; Hebrews 4:12).[41] Unlike the NDErs who casually interact with the being of light, John testifies,

> When I saw him, I fell at his feet as though dead. Then he placed his right hand on me and said: "Do not be afraid. I am the First and the Last. I am the Living One; I was dead, and behold I am alive for ever and ever! And I hold the keys of death and Hades" (Revelation 1:17,18).

This revelation of the exalted Jesus Christ is a far cry from the morally indifferent being of light so often described in NDEs. This Jesus has absolute ethical authority. Unlike Betty Eadie,[42] John didn't claim to be "worthy" of the living Christ, even though he knew he had been forgiven of his sins (Revelation 1:5). John fell headlong before Christ, prostrate in *worship*. Eadie says nothing about worshiping Jesus in *Embraced by the Light*. After all, a person is not going to worship God if she thinks she is worthy of him.

A striking illustration of this is found in the story Jesus told about the Pharisee and the tax collector:

> Two men went up to the temple to pray, one a Pharisee and the other a tax collector. The Pharisee, standing by himself, was praying thus, "God, I thank you that I am not like other people: thieves, rogues, adulterers, or even like this tax collector. I fast twice a week; I give a tenth of all my income." But the tax collector, standing far off, would not even look up to heaven, but was beating his breast and saying, "God, be merciful to me, a sinner!" I tell you, this man went down to his home justified rather than the other; for all who exalt themselves will be humbled, but all who humble themselves will be exalted (Luke 18:10-14 NRSV).

An awareness of the contrast between human unworthiness and the awesome perfection of God does not appear in most NDEs. When, for example, P.M.H. (Phyllis) Atwater had a life-review during an NDE, she first experienced feelings of "sadness and failure," but then she realized that "Phyllis was okay."[43] Missing from such NDEs is the presence of a holy God who calls the NDEr's life into question on the basis of an ultimate standard of truth and goodness.

Carol Zaleski observes that although NDErs may feel "pangs of regret for misdeeds and missed opportunities, guilt, that anathema of humanistic psychology, has no place in the near-death reports."[44] The being of light "communicates, but never excommunicates."[45] Yet if human guilt before God is objectively real, such experiences can only be deceptive—either because they are subjective projections of the NDEr's imagination, or because they are spiritual deceptions wrought by the enemy of truth.

DEMONIC DECEPTION

Some people argue that such ennobling and inspiring feelings as were experienced by Betty Eadie and others could not be from Satan, who is totally evil. Raymond Moody reasons that if there were demonic involvement in these experiences, NDErs would return to pursue a life of obvious evil, which typically they do not. In fact, they often seem to become better people.[46] Such reasoning is naive. The apostle Paul cautioned the early Christians that "Satan himself masquerades as an angel of light. It is not surprising, then, if his servants masquerade as servants of righteousness" (2 Corinthians 11:14,15).

Jesus Christ claimed to be "the light of the world" (John 8:12), and he revealed himself to Paul and John in a shining radiance. Satan can mimic this to some degree in order to mislead the undiscerning, and Jesus warned that Satan tries to obscure the truth in a myriad of ways. What is genuine can be counterfeited; an original can be imitated, whether in the natural or the supernatural realm.

The apostle Paul also warned that fallen angelic beings can present a distorted view of Jesus (Galatians 1:8). Saint Augustine (354-430) wisely noted that demonic beings—angels who rebelled against God under the leadership of Satan (Jude 6; Matthew 25:41)—have been studying humans for millennia.

> The demons . . . through the long period into which
> their life is extended, have gained a far greater expe-
> rience in events than accrues to men because of the
> brief span of their lives. Through [their spiritual]
> faculties, demons not only foretell many things that
> will occur, but also perform many miraculous acts.[47]

The manifestation of psychic powers is a case in point. Whether
they occur during and/or after an NDE, their occurrence is no
guarantee that the experience is from God. The key for discernment is to discover whether or not the spiritual message of
the NDE contradicts the teaching of Jesus. As we have seen,
many popular NDEs do precisely this. Moreover, an NDE can
be spiritually deceptive even if it does not involve a being of
light or psychic phenomena.

If Satan or one of his ministers could deceive someone into
thinking he had encountered a Christlike being of light who
unconditionally accepted him, this would instill a false sense of
peace and security. It is one thing to *feel* forgiven or accepted; it
is quite another thing to *be* forgiven and accepted. The difference spans the gap between heaven and hell.

A psychic or paranormal effect does not ensure that the NDE
has put someone in touch with God, even if the impression of
divinity is given. Psychic effects are produced by deceptive
spiritual agents who have two main strategies: to downgrade
God's holiness in order to make him seem less intrusive and
demanding, and to upgrade the moral stature of humans so
they seem worthy of God (as Eadie teaches) or even divine
themselves (as Ring teaches). These strategies break down the
perception of a need for a divine intermediary between a holy
God and a sinful people (1 Timothy 2:5).

For some reason, Betty Eadie, unlike many NDErs, grants
the reality of Satan and demons. But she seems completely
oblivious to the possibility that she might have been deceived

by them. Some NDEs may very well involve the presence of spirit beings who dazzle those who encounter them; but perception without discernment is dangerous. The AIDS virus appears fascinating in its complexity when viewed through a microscope, but it is deadly in its ultimate effects on the unknowing. One church father keenly observed:

> The idea that there is anything especially important in the sensuous perception of spirits is a mistaken one. Sensuous perception without spiritual perception does not provide a proper understanding of spirits; it provides only a superficial understanding of them. Very easily it can provide the most mistaken conceptions, and this indeed is what is most often provided to the inexperienced and to those infected with vainglory and self-esteem.[48]

Even occult literature reports that spirit beings can take on deceiving identities. Robert E. Monroe, a close associate of Elisabeth Kubler-Ross and Raymond Moody,[49] has had numerous OBEs, and he even trains people to induce them. He also has written several books on the subject. During an OBE that did not involve an NDE, Monroe observed "two little fellows" who had the ability to transform themselves at will, each of which "turned into a good facsimile of one of my two daughters."[50] Likewise, Sri Chinmoy, an Eastern guru and medium, speaks of deceptive spirits who impersonate one's guru in visions and even compel followers to kill themselves.[51] Such observations harmonize with Paul's warning that Satan and his agents (demons) can transform themselves for purposes of deception (2 Corinthians 11:14,15).[52]

Seraphim Rose rightly observes that the NDE is not an "after-death" experience but a " 'first moment of death' state," which is only the "antechamber to other much more extensive experiences" that occur at biological death.[53] And the antechamber may be decorated with deception and inhabited by imitators. Rose also discerns that, unlike the scientific study of the "raw material" of the natural realm, the "raw material" of the spiritual realm between life and death is "hidden, extremely difficult to grasp, and, in many cases, *has a will of its own*—a will to deceive the observer."[54] What you see may not be what you ultimately get. What you see may be what gets you.

The NDE does give us a glimpse of vast and varying spiritual dimensions, but it is not a realm that is easily navigated or readily fathomed. By virtue of our spiritual ignorance and moral limitations, the spiritual environments encountered in the NDE may seduce instead of illuminate.[55] This realm is not the final state of the soul, but an intermediary state of detachment from the body and engagement with an immaterial but not wholly benign spiritual reality.

10

AFTEREFFECTS

Our Savior, Christ Jesus, . . . has destroyed death and has brought life and immortality to light through the gospel.

—The apostle Paul (1 Timothy 1:10)

Breathtaking accounts of wonderful worlds beyond death's door are mesmerizing millions today. Those individuals impressed and inspired by books like Betty Eadie's *Embraced by the Light* are led to believe that all is well on the other side, that our weary race's perennial fear of death is unfounded. The welcoming light awaits us all . . . or so we are told.

My burden in writing this study of near-death experiences has been to caution fellow mortals about their prospects for immortality. The certainty of our mortality sparks hope for immortality. We are all exiled from Eden and yearning for heaven. But yearning for heaven is not the same as possessing it; wishing does not make it so. Some people may have been deceived by the light.

We have learned that some NDEs are real experiences of the spiritual world, and that they indicate the soul can exist apart from the body. However, this does not guarantee that all NDEs reveal the truth about the afterlife. C.S. Lewis warned, "We should never ask of anything, 'Is it real?' . . . The proper question is 'A real *what?*' "[1] We've discovered that NDErs give varying reports about the afterlife, and that these reports cannot all be true.

Furthermore, the teachings of Jesus and the Bible warn us to beware of spiritual deception that can lull us into a false security about our eternal destiny. It is possible to have a near-death experience of a spiritual entity or entities who feel no obligation to lead one into truth. It is far better to trust the word of the One who has conquered death through his matchless resurrection than to rely on the reports of the resuscitated.

In assessing an account of a near-death experience, several questions should be asked:

1. Is there good evidence that the person clinically died, or could this be a fabrication? Those who haven't died can't give firsthand reports about a place that is visited *after* death.

2. How does the NDEr describe his or her experience? Is biblical terminology used? If so, is it used in a biblically faithful way, or does the NDEr twist Scripture and distort its meaning, as Peter warned us about (2 Peter 3:16; 2:1-3)?

3. Does the NDEr present his or her experience as a new revelation that adds to or contradicts the Scriptures? If so, it should be critically evaluated in light of biblical teaching (2 Timothy 3:15-17; Revelation 22:18,19).

4. What is the fruit of the NDEr's life? Does he or she truly glorify God by confessing Jesus Christ as Savior and Lord, or does he or she proclaim some other religious vision, such as New Age spirituality? Jesus said, "By their fruit you will recognize them" (Matthew 7:16).

In a precarious world, we are all "near death." According to Jesus, this means we are all either near hell or near heaven. If we trust the no-risk, Pollyanna theology of so many popular writers and NDErs, we will fail to assess our prospects for immortality with sufficient caution. Jesus warned that one's soul can be lost if not entrusted to the true and living God (Matthew 16:26).

If an infinitely holy and all-knowing being were to inspect your life, what would he uncover? "Nothing in all creation is hidden from God's sight. Everything is uncovered and laid bare before the eyes of him to whom we must give account" (Hebrews 4:13). If the risen Christ were in charge of your "life-review" at the last judgment, how would he respond? Does God grade on a curve? The Bible denies it. Jesus' life, teaching, death, and resurrection provide a far firmer foundation for eternal life than trusting in one's own goodness, one's own divinity, or God's leniency.

The only sure basis for an endless life of joy is the gospel message. Despite our unworthiness and guilt before God, God loved us enough to provide forgiveness of our sins through the atoning death of Jesus on the cross. By repenting of our sins and turning toward the risen Christ in faith, we can receive the gift of everlasting life, beginning now and continuing into eternity (1 John 5:11,12). Jesus Christ suffered and died on the cross that we might be freed from the fear of death and hell. Jesus Christ rose from the dead to offer heaven to all who heed his call. He said, "I am the resurrection and the life. He who believes in me will live, even though he dies; and whoever lives and believes in me will never die" (John 11:25).

The book of Revelation depicts Jesus as the "Lamb" who was slain, and who is the source of joy for his followers in the paradise to come.

> Never again will they hunger; never again will they thirst. The sun will not beat upon them, nor any scorching heat. For the Lamb at the center of the throne will be their shepherd; he will lead them to springs of living water. And God will wipe away every tear from their eyes (Revelation 7:16,17).

Near the end of the book of Revelation, John invites all to partake of this eternal fellowship with the Lamb and his followers. "The Spirit and the bride [the church] say, 'Come!' And let him who hears say, 'Come!' Whoever is thirsty, let him come; and whoever wishes, let him take the free gift of the water of life" (Revelation 22:17).

Don't be lured by a deceptive light devoid of truth, when reality for the redeemed is as wonderful as this.

Appendix

IS IT ALL IN THE BRAIN?

*I cannot believe that the gift of conscious experience
has no further future, no possibility of another existence
under some intangible conditions. At least I would maintain that this possibility of a future existence cannot be
denied on scientific grounds.*

—Sir John Eccles, brain scientist

In reading the words of this book you have been using the most
sophisticated organ known—the two handfuls of living gray
matter called the brain. Although such processes as thinking,
seeing, hearing, tasting, and basic motor functions are usually
taken for granted, they all involve the proper working of an
organ that makes the most complicated computer look like a
Tinkertoy.

When our brains are in good repair, we stand a good chance
of perceiving reality accurately. Yet if we are fatigued, our
attention wanes. If we are medicated, abusing drugs, or with-
drawing from an addictive substance, we may hallucinate. As a
result, this most marvelous of physical endowments may play
tricks on us. We may take a deceptive, subjective experience
("it *seems* real") to be an authentic, objective reality ("it *is*
real"). Is this what happens in the NDE?

Twenty years ago the NDE was not a recognized subject of

study in medicine, psychology, or religion. There were scattered reports of NDEs before Moody's *Life After Life*, but the medical and scientific community did not have a ready name for these experiences or a typology of what they involved. Many dismissed the NDE as an invention. Today that has all changed.

The idea that the NDE is merely a fabrication of prankster patients or of money-hungry authors is no longer plausible. The integrity of research done by Michael Sabom and others has ruled out the likelihood of invention or sensationalism. It has been well established that NDEs occur fairly frequently (but not to all who clinically die), and that NDErs report similar experiences (but without uniform agreement). There is even a scholarly journal, *The Journal for Near-Death Studies*, dedicated to a better understanding of this phenomenon.

Nevertheless, the *objective reality* of the NDE is much disputed in scientific circles. Most people who have NDEs believe that they are objectively real. The question is whether or not this belief is correct. Do the distinctive elements of the NDE really occur as they are perceived, or are they the result of the abnormal functioning of the brain? Did the NDEr really traverse a tunnel toward a being of light, or can this be better explained apart from any spiritual dimension?

Researchers such as Moody, Ring, Sabom, and Morse—who affirm the existence of a spiritual realm—have attempted to counter the skeptics' arguments that the NDE is based merely on natural factors and does not involve the soul experiencing realities beyond the body. According to Melvin Morse, "Near-death studies have become the target of reductionism because many researchers are frustrated at not being able to explain this spiritual phenomenon."[1] Because the prevailing worldview of science tends to be materialism—the premise being that there is no spiritual realm but only material reality—it is quite common for scientists to try to explain any seemingly supernatural experience in natural terms according to known scientific laws.

In chapter 4, we argued that some OBEs associated with the NDE are verifiable and resist the natural explanations offered for them. However, several other objections to the NDE as an objectively real spiritual experience remain to be considered.

DRUGS ON THE BRAIN?

One nonspiritual explanation considers the effects of drugs on the brain. Certain drugs can cause hallucinations, and seriously ill patients may be heavily medicated with such hallucinogenic drugs. Some researchers, therefore, contend that NDEs are no more than hallucinations of the critically ill.

There are, for example, similarities between the LSD experience and the NDE. Both may involve an OBE, abnormal perceptions, and spiritual sensitivity. However, LSD experiences are often filled with distorted perceptions and a sense of unreality, whereas NDErs claim that their experiences were undistorted and real.[2] Furthermore, patients are not likely to take LSD in critical medical situations. Some patients might experience "flashbacks" triggered by previous uses of LSD, but this would account for only a tiny percentage of NDEs.

Morphine and heroin can also cause blissful hallucinations, but they are not usually interpreted as being real. These narcotics frequently cause a decrease in awareness, as well as physical side effects such as nausea, vomiting, and drowsiness, which are not associated with NDEs. Furthermore, narcotic hallucinations "do not involve traveling up a tunnel, seeing the Light, or having concrete visions of spirits, heaven, or God."[3]

Morse argues that hashish and other recreational drugs such as marijuana, cocaine, PCP, amphetamines, and barbiturates do not cause NDEs. Citing an unspecified Stanford University study, he writes that hashish and marijuana tend to induce "disorientation, speech disturbances, loss of control of thoughts, poor memory, depression, and outright fear."[4] Morse claims never to have seen these characteristics in NDE patients, though he seems to be discounting the negative NDEs we described in chapter 5, which included feelings of hopelessness and fear.

In order to discover if medically prescribed drugs could trigger an NDE, Morse interviewed "thirty-seven children who had been treated with almost every kind of mind-altering medication known to pharmacology," including "anesthetic agents, narcotics, Valium, Thorazine, Haldol, Dilantin, antidepressants, mood elevators, and pain killers." None of them had had anything resembling an NDE.[5] While Morse claims that other "anesthetic agents, such as halothane, surital, nitrous oxide, narcotics, and Nembutal, simply do not cause hallucinations,"[6] Moody records an OBE induced through nitrous oxide that bore some similarity to an NDE.[7] Even so, differences remain between the drug-induced experiences and the NDE.[8]

An anesthetic called ketamine was once thought of as an NDE trigger. Ketamine is known to produce an autoscopic, or self-visualizing, hallucination.[9] This is a strange occurrence, in which a mirror-image of one's self is observed without benefit of a mirror. It can also be brought on by depression, epilepsy, or schizophrenia. Yet the autoscopic hallucination differs from the OBE that occurs in many NDEs, in that: 1) the physical body observes a projected image or double, 2) the experiencer interacts with the double, 3) the double is perceived as unreal, and 4) these experiences are commonly negative.[10] Because ketamine hallucinations are normally frightening, it is no longer used as an anesthetic.

Susan Blackmore notes that if NDEs were drug-induced hallucinations, "you might expect that the deepest and most vivid NDEs would happen to people who were taking drugs at the time. This is clearly not the case. . . . Drug intoxication during a close brush with death actually diminishes the chance of an NDE . . . [and researchers] suggest that drug-free NDEs diverge more from the normal state of consciousness than drug-inhibited NDEs."[11] Furthermore, patients who have experienced both drug-induced hallucinations and NDEs report that they are very different experiences.[12]

Carol Zaleski observes that although some aspects of the NDE can be duplicated through drugs, "one cannot build a coherent theory of near-death experience on a psychopharmacological basis; not all near-death subjects were under medication, and in any case, the effects of different drugs vary endlessly."[13]

PSYCHOLOGICAL EXPLANATIONS

Those interested in debunking a spiritual explanation for the NDE have two other naturalistic explanations up their sleeves. The first appeals to psychological factors. The second is the physiological account that sees the dying brain as a closed theater of the cranium in which the NDE is played out.

Well-known astronomer and pundit Carl Sagan has a clever psychological interpretation of the NDE:

> The only alternative, so far as I can see, is that every human being, without exception, has already shared an experience like that of those travelers who return from the land of death: the sensation of flight; the emergence from darkness into light; an experience in which, at least sometimes, a heroic figure can be dimly perceived, bathed in radiance and glory. There is only one common experience that matches this description. It is called birth.[14]

In other words, the NDE is nothing but a reawakening during clinical death of the repressed memory of the birth experience.

Sagan's cleverness aside, the dissimilarities between physical birth and the NDE are too great for his argument to work.

First, it is unlikely that the newborn's perceptual abilities would be sufficiently mature to record the birth experience for recall during a later mortal crisis. Second, the birth canal is quite unlike the NDE tunnel. The infant doesn't float gracefully from the womb to the delivery room! The baby is in for a rough, tough, tight, and convulsive ride. And since the infant's eyes are pressed tightly against the birth canal, there is no sight of the light until arrival.[15]

Third, not all people leave the womb through the birth canal; some are delivered by Caesarean section. Blackmore found that the same percentage (36 percent) of NDErs born by Caesarean experienced the tunnel as did those born naturally.[16] Moreover, I have yet to hear of an NDE that involved perceiving a medical doctor as a "heroic figure bathed in radiance and glory." In fact, the reverse is the case. Doctors, as we have seen, may be observed by the NDEr, but they are often left behind in favor of the transfixing luminosity at the end of the tunnel.

Another naturalistic explanation has been called "transient depersonalization," the there-but-not-there phenomenon. Russell Noyes and others have shown that in the face of a perceived life-threatening situation, people switch into a kind of psychological emergency gear in order to function more effectively during the crisis. This may involve an altered sense of time, a feeling of detachment, quickened thought, a feeling of unreality, a lack of emotion, provoked memories (even a life-review), a sense of unity with the universe, or more acute vision or hearing. Noyes argues that the awareness of imminent death triggers these perceptions, some of which resemble aspects of an NDE.

Yet Sabom points out that many NDEs take place without any awareness of extreme danger, as in sudden deaths. Without warning, one of his patients clinically died of a heart attack and experienced an NDE, which he related after resuscitation. Furthermore, Noyes's theory only accounts for conscious cases in extreme situations, not cases in which people are unconscious because of clinical death.[17] Neither does it account for some other aspects of the NDE, such as visions of deceased relatives.[18]

A less sophisticated but initially plausible explanation is that the NDE results from a deep expectation and yearning for life after death. According to this view, the NDEr is psychologically primed for a particular experience. This expectation is triggered by a life-threatening situation and is manifested as a dream or hallucination.

Though NDE researchers emphasize that personal expectations and cultural conditioning can play a part in how NDEs are described, wish-fulfillment cannot explain the many cases in which NDEs do not conform to what patients expected. Sabom found this in a significant number of his interviews. One man previously thought that "when you're dead, you're dead." After his NDE, he believed that "your spirit does leave your body" at death.[19] Sabom asked his subjects what they would have thought if someone had related NDEs to them prior to their own. Many responded that they would have derided and dismissed them.[20] In an NDE noted in chapter 6, a being of light told a surprised woman that she was Jewish. Moreover, even if one subjectively desires something to occur (like consciousness after clinical death), this doesn't rule out the possibility that it *will* objectively occur. All in all, the wishful-thinking explanation fails to explain NDEs comprehensively.

Others argue that the NDE is a form of psychosis, which is a radical break with reality. Psychosis involves hallucinations, delusions (false beliefs irrationally held, like believing one is Napoleon), and loose associations (when one jumps from thought to thought without discernible order).[21] Moody, who holds an M.D. in psychiatry, has addressed this at some length. He first considers whether the NDE is a schizophrenia-related psychosis. Schizophrenics suffer from auditory hallucinations ("hearing voices"), strange mannerisms, loose associations, an inability to make sense of their experiences and thoughts, progressive apathy, and often a disengagement from society. Although NDErs sometimes hear voices, they always make some sense of the experience (however mysterious), and they usually view it as very positive or even life-changing. As we have seen, there is a basic coherence to most NDEs, even to the negative ones.

Moody illustrates the difference between schizophrenia and the NDE by comparing two of his interviews: the schizophrenic was disoriented and incoherent, while the NDEr clearly related her extraordinary experience. Moody also mentions that when NDErs have OBEs, they are not out of touch with their environment but observing it. Moreover, OBEs have been verified by family members and medical personnel.[22]

Moody also tackles the idea that the NDE results from an organic brain disorder called delirium, which is caused by a lack of oxygen and a chemical imbalance in the brain. The delirious tend to have fragmented and incoherent hallucinatory experiences that usually are not remembered clearly. Those suffering delirium view their experiences as delusive and not as spiritually significant. They also fail to report elements common to NDEs, such as the OBE, panoramic memory (or life-review), overwhelming feelings of love, and so forth.[23]

THE THEATER OF
THE DYING BRAIN?

Although Moody clearly differentiates NDEs from cases of delirium, Susan Blackmore believes that the NDE can be accounted for by oxygen abnormalities in the brain along with other physical factors. Her book *Dying to Live: Near-Death Experiences* (1993) is the most thorough and well-reasoned account to date that endeavors to explain the NDE comprehensively on the basis of neurological functions that occur under crisis conditions. Although I cannot do justice to the complexity of all her arguments, I will survey and respond to her main points.

Unlike other researchers who try to account for the entire NDE on the basis of one nonspiritual factor or another, Blackmore argues that each of the distinctive elements of the NDE is caused by a separate condition in the brain, which is not attributable to externally administered drugs. She believes that the various components of the NDE can occur in situations without clinical death, but that the combination of these components is unique to the NDE.[24]

Oxygen deprivation. Blackmore admits that we don't have direct knowledge of "what happens to the brain when a person approaches death"; doctors are busy saving the lives of patients who are near death and do not have opportunity to experiment on their brains at that time.[25] But we do know that at some point in the process of dying, the brain will stop receiving enough oxygen to function. Blackmore argues that oxygen deficiency in the brain explains critical aspects of the NDE.

In presenting this theory, Blackmore responds to several arguments that have been advanced against the idea that oxygen deprivation causes the NDE. First, there is the argument that NDEs can occur when oxygen deprivation is not a factor. She grants this, but dismisses it as a bad argument against her theory, because the NDE may have multiple causes. "The fact that NDEs can occur without anoxia [lack of oxygen in the brain] is no argument against it sometimes being responsible for them."[26]

This is true enough, but it fails to make the case that Blackmore wants to make, namely, that the NDE can be explained on the basis of physiological factors alone. Establishing the plausibility of a physical cause (anoxia) does not eliminate the possibility of a spiritual cause. For example, I could hallucinate that I was talking to the pope, but this wouldn't rule out the possibility that I might actually speak with the pope sometime. Furthermore, Blackmore's oxygen-deprivation theory is central and crucial to her entire explanation of the NDE. She believes that the tunnel experience, the noise, and the perception of light are all caused by lack of oxygen in the brain. For her theory to work, oxygen deprivation must be able to serve as the sole cause of these key elements of the NDE. (As we will see, Blackmore does propose other causes to explain other elements of the NDE.)

A second argument that has been advanced against the oxygen-deprivation theory points to evidence that one NDEr's blood oxygen level remained normal during his NDE.[27] Sabom recorded a case in which a man suffered a cardiac arrest, died, and had an NDE. During this time a blood sample was taken that indicated a relatively normal oxygen level. Sabom concluded that oxygen deficiency could not have been the cause of this NDE.[28]

But Blackmore argues that even though the blood gases in the patient's arteries were normal, the amount of oxygen in his *brain* could still have been depleted. Given the physiology that Blackmore describes, her point is well taken.

> If the heart stops pumping blood then blood in the arteries is not reaching the tissues or cells which will use it and therefore oxygen levels in those arteries will only fall very slowly. If extra oxygen is given as well, which is common during cardiac arrest, then the arterial levels may actually rise. By contrast, blood in the veins will not have much oxygen left because it is in contact with the tissues and

therefore loses oxygen. Since the brain uses a lot of oxygen, levels in the cerebral veins will fall fast and the brain quickly run out of the oxygen it needs. Sabom's patient had arterial blood tested and so we cannot conclude that he was not suffering from cerebral anoxia.[29]

However, even if it has not been established that oxygen levels in the brain remain normal during an NDE, it does not necessarily follow that a loss of oxygen in the brain accounts for key elements of the NDE.

A third argument against the oxygen-deprivation explanation is that it "causes effects quite unlike NDEs."[30] But there are various kinds of anoxia, depending on the speed of oxygen loss. Blackmore grants that an extremely fast or extremely slow loss of oxygen does not produce NDE-like symptoms; but intermediately rapid oxygen loss, combined with the accompanying rise in carbon dioxide, can create these kinds of symptoms.

Blackmore also argues that this kind of anoxia can cause the disinhibition (or excitation) of brain cells (which has been shown in rats), thus causing the "excitation of whole brain areas."[31] The excitation of cells in the region of the visual cortex in the brain could account for the perception of a tunnel and the light at the end of it. The random firing of the oxygen-starved cells can trigger the cortical area to produce a "flickering speckled world which gets brighter and brighter toward the centre."[32]

Although this could explain the light so often seen in the NDE, it cannot explain the intense feelings of calm and warmth. Neither does her theory explain the personification of the light as a being of light, which is a feature in many NDEs.

Endorphin release. To explain the bliss of NDE experiences, Blackmore appeals to the endorphin-release theory. Endorphins are chemicals naturally found in the brain that have a

morphine-like effect when activated. They explain the transition from agony to ecstasy that is felt in "the runner's high"
and in other extremely taxing physical situations, which she
argues are similar to conditions present during the onset of an
NDE. Blackmore maintains that endorphins are released to
counteract the extreme stress of dying, and so produce the
positive psychological effects found in most NDEs. Morse,
however, notes:

> There is no evidence in the medical literature that
> the stresses of dying actually produce significantly
> greater amounts of endorphins in the brain. In stud-
> ies of animals dying of bacteria on the brain, small
> amounts of these chemicals are documented, yet
> their significance is unclear.
>
> Most animal studies indicate that the brain be-
> comes depleted of these endorphins, which makes
> sense since their main function is to alleviate pain
> and therefore would be depleted quickly. No evi-
> dence exists to prove that the dying brain makes
> large quantities of these chemicals.[33]

Sabom also disputes that endorphins account for the positive feelings of the NDE. He cites an experiment in which beta-
endorphin was injected into the spinal fluid of 14 patients who
had intractable pain due to cancer. (Blackmore refers to beta-
endorphin as "the most powerful narcotic" among the endorphins.)[34] All patients were pain-free for between 22 and 73
hours. But in NDE cases, freedom from pain only occurs during the NDE itself (which lasts only a few moments). NDErs
often report intense pain upon returning to their bodies. One
man interviewed by Sabom said, "I was hurting real bad. . . .
But all of a sudden the pain completely stopped and I could feel
myself rising out of my body. . . . Then I started floating back

down to my body. As soon as I got down to my body, the pain came back. Tremendous pain."[35] Reports such as this are common.

Blackmore's theory requires a massive release of endorphins to generate bliss in the face of death and also to trigger hallucinations. Yet NDErs are not free from pain for the length of time that would be expected, assuming that the amount of endorphin injected into the cancer patients was roughly equivalent to the amount that would be released naturally in the face of death. Furthermore, the majority of the cancer patients injected with beta-endorphin experienced drowsiness and sleep. This "does not fit with the state of 'hyperalertness' described in the NDE, in which there is a clarity of 'vision' and thought."[36] Sabom also noted that the cancer patients continued to have a sense of touch, while NDErs lose it after leaving their bodies. One woman reported to Sabom that during her NDE she felt no sensation as she watched a physician insert an IV into her arm.[37]

In conclusion, the endorphin-release theory is far from substantiated as an explanation for the feelings of peace and well-being that often accompany the NDE. It is debatable whether endorphins are released during NDEs. If they are released it is far from clear that they would have all the effects that Blackmore's theory requires. Even if endorphins do induce a kind of euphoria, this emotional state is not the same as feeling acceptance and love, as is often reported in NDEs. Furthermore, endorphin release could not account for the negative feelings of hell-like NDEs.

Blackmore thinks that hellish NDEs are so infrequent that they don't merit much concern, although she briefly suggests two explanations for them. Either they are caused by the drug naloxone, or they are hallucinations caused by violent resuscitation activity.[38] In chapter 5, we criticized the latter idea (held by D. Scott Rogo) as inadequate. And naloxone would not explain all hell-like experiences, many of which occur without the administration of the drug. Moreover, hell-like NDEs are common enough to take seriously.

Blackmore believes endorphins also account for the NDE life-review. Endorphins are known to "lower the threshold of seizures in the limbic system and the temporal lobe. The resulting abnormal activity in the temporal lobe causes the flashbacks and associated feelings of familiarity and meaningfulness," as well as the sense of timelessness so often reported in NDEs.[39] As usual, she gives careful, well-documented arguments for her theory. But, as I argued above, if endorphins are not released in the manner Blackmore claims, the explanation fails.

Ego dissolution. Blackmore proposes that the transformative effects of the NDE are caused by the breakup of the self, which she believes occurs during the NDE. This frees a person from the illusion of an individual ego and provides a sense of liberation. She bases this idea primarily on the Buddhist view of the self as unreal.[40]

Let us consider three objections. First, few NDErs claim to experience a breakup of the self or to attribute their personal transformation to this as a cause. Second, if NDErs were to experience the breakup of the self, *who* would come back to tell of it?[41] Third, unlike the rest of her book, Blackmore's explanation at this point is more philosophically speculative than it is physiologically verifiable. As such, it is more dependent on the philosophical credibility of Buddhism than it is on empirical evidence.

THE SPIRITUAL FACTOR REMAINS

How, then, can we reasonably evaluate the attempt to discredit all NDEs scientifically? Is the NDE all in the brain? To handle every detail of every argument would take a book in itself, but I believe that all NDEs cannot be explained away on the basis of natural factors, even if some aspects of some NDEs are susceptible to merely physical explanations. In particular, the verifiable out-of-the-body experiences, as discussed in chapter 4, are inexplicable solely on natural grounds. The near-death experience proves to be a challenge to the materialism of modern science, just as it challenges those who are spiritually inclined to interpret its meaning properly.

BIBLIOGRAPHY

Abanes, Richard. *"Embraced by the Light" and the Bible: Betty Eadie and Near-Death Experiences in the Light of Scripture*. Camp Hill, PA: Horizon Books, 1994. 241 pp. An in-depth analysis of Betty Eadie's views and background, as well as other material on the near-death experience.

Anderson, J. Kerby. *Life, Death, and Beyond*. Grand Rapids, MI: Zondervan Publishing House, 1980. 205 pp. One of the first careful treatments of the near-death experience from a Christian viewpoint.

Ankerberg, John, and John Weldon. *The Facts on Life After Death*. Eugene, OR: Harvest House, 1992. 48 pp. A helpful booklet assessing NDEs from a biblical perspective.

Ankerberg, John, and John Weldon. *The Coming Darkness*. Eugene, OR: Harvest House, 1993. 342 pp. Details the dangers of all manner of occult involvement, much of which relates to NDE phenomena.

Atwater, P.M.H. *Coming Back to Life: The After-Effects of the Near-Death Experience*. 1988. Reprint. New York: Ballantine Books, 1989. 262 pp. One of the first studies by someone with a New Age orientation to address negative NDEs.

Atwater, P.M.H. *Beyond the Light: What Isn't Being Said About Near-Death Experience*. New York: Birch Lane Press, 1994. 296 pp. An extensive analysis.

Blackmore, Susan. *Dying to Live: Near-Death Experiences*. Buffalo, NY: Prometheus Books, 1993. 291 pp. A skeptical analysis from an atheistic position. Very carefully argued.

Brinkley, Dannion, with Paul Perry. *Saved by the Light*. New York: Villard Books, 1994. 162 pp. An extended account of the author's two near-death experiences from an essentially New Age perspective.

Eadie, Betty J., with Curtis Taylor. *Embraced by the Light*. Placerville, CA: Gold Leaf Press, 1992. 147 pp. A detailed account of a near-death experience from a Mormon-New Age perspective.

Groothuis, Douglas. *Unmasking the New Age: Is There a New Religious Movement Trying to Transform Society?* Downers Grove, IL: InterVarsity Press, 1986. 192 pp.

Groothuis, Douglas. *Confronting the New Age: How to Resist a Growing Religious Movement*. Downers Grove, IL: InterVarsity Press, 1988. 230 pp.

Groothuis, Douglas. *Revealing the New Age Jesus: Challenges to Orthodox Views of Christ*. Downers Grove, IL: InterVarsity Press, 1990. 264 pp. Although not directly concerned with NDEs, *Unmasking*, *Confronting*, and *Revealing* address matters relevant to the worldview that emerges from many NDEs.

Habermas, Gary R., and J.P. Moreland. *Immortality: the Other Side of Death*. Nashville, TN: Thomas Nelson, 1992. 275 pp. An in-depth analysis of the philosophical and theological issues of death and dying from a Christian orientation.

Moody, Raymond A., Jr. *Life After Life*. 1975. Reprint. New York: Bantam Books, 1976. 187 pp. The book that opened the doors to serious study of the NDE. Written from a syncretistic viewpoint.

Moody, Raymond A., Jr. *Reflections on Life After Life*. 1977. Reprint. New York: Bantam Books, 1978. 146 pp. A follow-up to *Life After Life*.

Moody, Raymond A., Jr., with Paul Perry. *The Light Beyond*. New York: Bantam Books, 1988. 205 pp. More explorations of the NDE, including material on NDEs in children.

Morey, Robert A. *Death and the Afterlife*. Minneapolis, MN: Bethany House Publishers, 1984. 315 pp. A thorough study of the biblical position and its rivals.

Morse, Melvin, with Paul Perry. *Closer to the Light: Learning from the Near-Death Experiences of Children*. 1990. Reprint. New York: Ivy Books, 1991. 236 pp. The first major study of NDEs in children. Presented from a generally New Age angle.

Morse, Melvin, with Paul Perry. *Transformed by the Light: The Powerful Effect of Near-Death Experiences on People's Lives*. 1992. Reprint. New York: Ivy Books, 1994. 265 pp. A study of the spiritual effects of the NDE in adults.

Probasco, William L. *The Lie at the End of the Tunnel: A Critique of "Embraced by the Light."* Gadsden, AL: Church Ministry Resources, 1994. 55 pp. A Christian analysis concerned mostly with Mormon connections.

Rawlings, Maurice. *Beyond Death's Door*. 1978. Reprint. New York: Bantam Books, 1979. 157 pp. Offers several accounts of NDEs he encountered after reviving patients. A Christian orientation. Rawlings was the first to report negative NDEs.

Rawlings, Maurice. *To Hell and Back: Life After Death, Startling New Evidence*. Nashville, TN: Thomas Nelson Publishers, 1993. 255 pp. A sequel to *Beyond*.

Ring, Kenneth. *Life at Death: A Scientific Investigation of the Near-Death Experience*. New York: Coward, McCann, and Geoghegan, 1980. 310 pp. The first scientific investigation of the NDE. Written from a New Age viewpoint.

Ring, Kenneth. *Heading Toward Omega: In Search of the Meaning of the Near-Death Experience*. 2nd ed. New York: Quill, 1985. 348 pp. A mystical elaboration on *Life at Death* that explores the spiritual significance of the NDE for planetary changes.

Ring, Kenneth. *The Omega Project: Near-Death Experiences, UFO Encounters, and Mind at Large*. New York: Quill, 1992. 320 pp. Ties in the NDE with other paranormal phenomena.

Ritchie, George G., with Elizabeth Sherrill. *Return from Tomorrow*. Grand Rapids, MI: Fleming H. Revell, Baker Book House, 1978. 124 pp. The NDE account that first interested Moody in the phenomenon. Written from a generally Christian perspective, although some material may not fit the biblical picture.

Rogo, D. Scott. *The Return from Silence: A Study of Near-Death Experiences*. Northamptonshire, England: The Aquarian Press, 1989. 256 pp. An analysis by a parapsychologist. Written from a basically New Age perspective.

Rose, Fr. Seraphim. *The Soul After Death*. Platina, CA: Saint Herman of Alaska Brotherhood, 1980. 296 pp. An earlier study of the NDE from an Eastern Orthodox perspective.

Sabom, Michael B. *Recollections of Death: A Medical Investigation*. New York: Harper and Row, 1982. 224 pp. One of the first scientific studies of the NDE. Does not take an overt religious position. A very thorough and fair treatment.

Swihart, Phillip J. *The Edge of Death*. Downers Grove, IL: InterVarsity Press, 1978. 96 pp. A brief Christian critique.

Wilson, Ian. *The After Death Experience*. New York: Quill, 1987. 234 pp. A journalistic investigation that covers a variety of paranormal phenomena relating to the afterlife, including the NDE.

Zaleski, Carol. *Otherworld Journeys: Accounts of Near-Death Experience in Medieval and Modern Times*. New York: Oxford University Press, 1987. 275 pp. A scholarly study that reaches no firm conclusions on the actual nature of the NDE.

NOTES

Chapter 1—Betty and the Light

1. Carol Zaleski, *Otherworld Journeys: Accounts of Near-Death Experience in Medieval and Modern Times* (New York: Oxford Press, 1987), 12.
2. Blaise Pascal, *Pensees*, translated with an introduction by A.J. Krailsheimer (New York: Penguin Books, 1966), #434/199, 165.
3. Melvin Morse, foreword to *Embraced by the Light*, by Betty Eadie with Curtis Taylor (Placerville, CA: Gold Leaf Press, 1992), xii.
4. Jim Jerome, "Heaven Can Wait," *People*, 11 October 1993, 81. This quote is from a caption under a picture of Eadie.
5. C.S. Lewis, *The Weight of Glory and Other Addresses*, revised and expanded edition (New York: Macmillan Publishing Co., 1980), 6-7.
6. Ibid., 15-16.
7. Eadie, *Embraced*, 40-42.
8. Ibid., 5-6.
9. Ibid., 9.
10. Ibid., 10.
11. Ibid., 11. Her teacher was violating the New Testament exhortation to "be merciful to those who doubt" (Jude 22).
12. Her response shows that she lacked the confidence that for the Christian the Second Coming is "the blessed hope—the glorious appearing of our great God and Savior, Jesus Christ" (Titus 2:13) and not something terrifying.
13. Eadie, *Embraced*, 12.
14. Ibid., 31-32.
15. Ibid., 39. This is a reference to David's words in Psalm 23:4, which do not speak of a condition *after* death but to one that threatens death. Being in "the shadow of death" means to be threatened with mortal danger. For instance, if I'm standing in the shadow of a house I'm not in the house. David certainly believed in life after death, but he was not describing it here.
16. Ibid., 45-46.
17. Dannion Brinkley's account of his NDE recorded in *Saved by the Light* (New York: Villard Books, 1994) is quite extraordinary as well. Although the book became a bestseller, it has not attained the celebrity status of Eadie's story. We will be discussing his account in the following chapters.
18. Eadie, *Embraced*, 45.
19. Ibid., 46.
20. Ibid., 47. Eadie is incorrect. Orthodox doctrine does not teach that Jesus and the Father are one being, but that they are two persons with one essence or substance. This will be addressed further in chapter 2.
21. Ibid., 49-50.
22. Ibid., 59.
23. Ibid., 61.
24. Ibid.
25. Ibid., 67.
26. Ibid., 70.

Chapter 2—How Christian Is It?

1. Betty J. Eadie with Curtis Taylor, *Embraced by the Light* (Placerville, CA: Gold Leaf Press, 1992), 85; emphasis in the original.

2. Richard Abanes, *"Embraced by the Light" and the Bible* (Camp Hill, PA: Horizon Books, 1994), 29.

3. Ibid., 28.

4. Ibid., 30; 217-20.

5. Ibid., 26-27.

6. From a radio interview with Al Kresta on WMUZ, Detroit, Michigan, on March 3, 1994. Partially transcribed in *Spiritual Counterfeits Journal* 18:4/19:1 (1994): 30.

7. Eadie, *Embraced*, 93.

8. Ibid., 43.

9. I owe this turn of phrase to a radio sermon by Charles Swindoll.

10. See the Mormon defense, Rex E. Lee, *What Do Mormons Believe?* (Salt Lake City, UT: Deseret Book Company, 1992), 21.

11. Eadie, *Embraced*, 110.

12. Ibid., 119; emphasis mine.

13. Ibid., 47.

14. See John Ankerberg and John Weldon, *Cult Watch: What You Need to Know About Spiritual Deception* (Eugene, OR: Harvest House, 1991), 26-28.

15. See Abanes, *"Embraced by the Light" and the Bible*, 51-52.

16. On refuting the Mormon doctrine of preexistence, see David A. Reed and John R. Farkas, *Mormons Answered Verse by Verse* (Grand Rapids, MI: Baker Book House, 1992), 57-58, 80-81.

17. See William L. Probasco, *The Lie At the End of the Tunnel: A Critique of "Embraced by the Light"* (Gadsden, AL: Church Ministry Resources, 1994), 17.

18. This belief is grounded largely in the Mormon scripture *The Pearl of Great Price* in the Book of Moses 3:5 and the Book of Abraham 3:21,22. On this see Ruth Tucker, *Another Gospel: Alternative Religions and the New Age Movement* (Grand Rapids, MI: Zondervan Publishing House, 1989), 82-83.

19. In Genesis 1:26, God says, "Let us make humankind in our image" (NRSV). However, this plural reference does not imply any preexistent spirits giving God a hand. It refers either to the Trinity or to God's declaration of his intention before the heavenly court of angels (see 1 Kings 22:19). Whichever is the case, verse 27 goes on to say that humans were created in God's image, not in the image of a committee of preexistent human spirits.

20. Interview with Hugh Downs on "20/20," ABC-TV, May 13, 1994.

21. For a Christian response to the problem of evil and suffering, see Winfried Corduan, *Reasonable Faith: Basic Christian Apologetics* (Nashville, TN: Broadman and Holland Publishers, 1993), 123-45; D.A. Carson, *How Long, Oh Lord? Reflections on Suffering and Evil* (Grand Rapids, MI: Baker Book House, 1990); and Millard Erickson, *The Word Made Flesh: A Contemporary Incarnational Christology* (Grand Rapids, MI: Baker Book House, 1991), 599-624.

22. Eadie, *Embraced*, 44.

23. Ibid., 97.

24. William Wordsworth, "Ode: Intimations of Immortality from Recollections of Early Childhood," quoted in John Newport, *Life's Ultimate Questions: A Contemporary Philosophy of Religion* (Dallas, TX: Word, 1989), 276.

25. Eadie, *Embraced*, 49-50.

26. Ibid., 70.
27. Ibid., 113.
28. Ibid., 94.
29. Ibid., 71.
30. Ibid., 109.
31. This point is documented in Craig Branch, "Clues to a Near Death Experience," *Spiritual Counterfeits Journal* 18:4/19:1 (1994): 37.
32. On Gnosticism, see Douglas Groothuis, *Revealing the New Age Jesus: Challenges to Orthodox Views of Christ* (Downers Grove, IL: InterVarsity Press, 1990), 73-118.
33. Eadie, *Embraced*, 45.
34. Ibid., 61.
35. Probasco, *The Lie*, explores this and many Mormon connections with Eadie's thought, as does Branch, "Clues," and Abanes, *"Embraced by the Light" and the Bible*, 25-82. For a good overview of Mormon doctrine and how it differs from biblical teaching, see Ankerberg and Weldon, *Cult Watch*, 9-52.
36. Eadie, *Embraced*, 41. For further discussion of New Age theology, see chapter 6.
37. Ibid., 81.
38. On the role of angels in near-death experiences, see Gary Kinnaman, *Angels: Dark and Light* (Ann Arbor, MI: Servant Publications, 1994), 99-110.
39. Ibid., 41.
40. C.S. Lewis, *The Weight of Glory and Other Addresses*, revised and expanded edition (New York: Macmillan Publishing Co., Inc., 1980), 13.
41. Eadie, *Embraced*, 70.
42. Ibid., 118; emphasis in the original.
43. Eadie claims her NDE taught her that male supremacy is divinely ordained. See Ibid., 110-11.
44. Ibid., 119.
45. Ibid., 131-32.
46. See Ibid., 67-68.
47. Written statement by Robert Bierma, June 9, 1994.

Chapter 3—What Happens in a Near-Death Experience?

1. Carol Zaleski, *Otherworld Journeys: Accounts of Near-Death Experience in Medieval and Modern Times* (New York: Oxford University Press, 1987), 30.
2. These kinds of explanations are addressed in more detail in the Appendix, "Is It All in the Brain?"
3. George G. Ritchie with Elizabeth Sherrill, *Return from Tomorrow* (Grand Rapids, MI: Fleming H. Revell, Baker Book House, 1994; orig. pub. 1978).
4. Elisabeth Kubler-Ross, foreword to *Life After Life*, by Raymond A. Moody, Jr. (1975; reprint, New York: Bantam, 1976), xi.
5. Andrew Greeley, foreword to *The Light Beyond*, by Raymond A. Moody, Jr., with Paul Perry (New York: Bantam Books, 1988), vii.
6. Moody, *Life*, 181.
7. Ibid., 184.
8. Ibid., 25.
9. See Ibid., 23-25, for the qualifications that Moody gives for the composite account.
10. Ibid., 27.

11. Eadie, *Embraced by the Light* (Placerville, CA: Gold Leaf Press, 1992), 4.
12. Moody, *Life*, 29.
13. Eadie, *Embraced*, 30.
14. Ibid., 29.
15. Ibid., 37.
16. Moody, *Life*, 30-34.
17. Eadie, *Embraced*, 37-39.
18. Ibid., 29.
19. Moody, *Life*, 55.
20. Ibid., 61.
21. Eadie, *Embraced*, 40-53.
22. Moody, *Life*, 71.
23. Eadie, *Embraced*, 112.
24. Moody, *Life*, 74.
25. Eadie, *Embraced*, 117-18.
26. Moody, *Life*, 84-85.
27. Ibid., 88-89.
28. Ibid., 92.
29. Ibid., 93.
30. Ibid., 91. This area has also been studied by physician Melvin Morse and others, which we will see in chapter 9.
31. Eadie, *Embraced*, 147.
32. Ibid., 146.
33. Moody, *Life*, 95.
34. Ibid., 97.
35. Ibid., 98.
36. Eadie, *Embraced*, 61.
37. Moody, *Life*, 99.
38. Ibid. We will explore this fascinating phenomenon in chapter 4.
39. Eadie, *Embraced*, 33-35.
40. Raymond A. Moody, Jr., *Reflections on Life After Life* (1977; reprint, New York: Bantam, 1978), 14.
41. Eadie, *Embraced*, 76-77.
42. Moody, *Reflections*, 17.
43. Eadie, *Embraced*, 72-130.
44. Moody, *Reflections*, 18-22.
45. Eadie, *Embraced*, 38.
46. Moody, *Reflections*, 27.
47. Eadie, *Embraced*, 126-27.
48. Moody, *Reflections*, 135-43.

Chapter 4—Scientific Investigations

1. Carol Zaleski, *Otherworld Journeys: Accounts of Near-Death Experience in Medieval and Modern Times* (New York: Oxford, 1987), 103. Raymond A. Moody, Jr., speaks of Sabom and Ring in his book, written with Paul Perry, *The Light Beyond* (New York: Bantam, 1988), 138-45 (Sabom) and 155-63 (Ring).
2. Zaleski, *Otherworld*, 104.

3. Kenneth Ring, *Life at Death: A Scientific Investigation of the Near-Death Experience* (New York: Coward, McCann, and Geoghegan, 1980), 17.

4. Ibid., 22.

5. Ibid., 40 (chart); yet on page 60, Ring says that "about one-fifth of our experiencer sample" entered the final stage. I cannot explain this discrepancy.

6. Ibid., 188-89.

7. Ibid., 185.

8. Ibid., 173-86.

9. Kenneth Ring, *Heading Toward Omega: In Search of the Meaning of the Near-Death Experience*, 2nd ed. (New York: William Morrow, 1985), 269.

10. This aspect of Ring's thinking will be discussed in more detail in chapter 9.

11. For an analysis of the New Age movement, see Douglas Groothuis, *Unmasking the New Age: Is There a New Religious Movement Trying to Transform Society?* (Downers Grove, IL: InterVarsity Press, 1986), and *Confronting the New Age: How to Resist a Growing Religious Movement* (Downers Grove, IL: InterVarsity Press, 1988). For a review of Deepak Chopra's popular New Age books, *Ageless Body, Timeless Mind: The Quantum Alternative to Growing Old* (1993) and *Perfect Health: The Complete Mind/ Body Guide* (1992), see John Weldon, "A Summary Critique," *Christian Research Journal* 16 (Winter 1994): 43-45.

12. Michael Sabom, *Recollections at Death: A Medical Investigation* (New York: Harper and Row Publishers, 1982), 10-13.

13. Ibid., 14-23.

14. Ibid., 24-37.

15. We will return to these claims later in the chapter.

16. Sabom, *Recollections*, 39-54.

17. Ibid., 52.

18. Ibid., 27.

19. Ibid., 61.

20. Ibid., 124.

21. Ibid., 124-25.

22. Ibid., 129-30.

23. Ibid., 130.

24. Ibid., 131.

25. Melvin Morse with Paul Perry, *Closer to the Light: Learning from the Near-Death Experiences of Children* (1990; reprint, New York: Ivy Books, 1991), 1-8. Morse notes on page 7 that Katie's family was Mormon, as is Betty Eadie. Although he doesn't mention it, Katie's vision of seeing souls waiting to be born agrees with the Mormon doctrine of the preexistence of the soul, as discussed with respect to Betty Eadie's NDE in chapter 2.

26. Ibid., 21. When Morse recounts the study in his second book, written with Paul Perry, *Transformed by the Light: The Powerful Effect of Near-Death Experiences on People's Lives* (1992; reprint, New York: Ivy Books, 1994), 24, he says the control group consisted of 176 children. I cannot explain the discrepancy in these two accounts.

27. Ibid., 23. Other studies challenge this finding. This will be discussed in chapter 7.

28. Morse, *Closer*, 40.

29. Ibid., 131.

30. Ibid., 135. Betty Eadie also speaks of death as "rebirth." See Betty J. Eadie with Curtis Taylor, *Embraced by the Light* (Placerville, CA: Gold Leaf Press, 1992), 31-32.

31. Morse, *Closer*, 137.
32. Ibid., 139-41.
33. Ibid., 106-30. Morse elaborates on this theory in *Transformed*, 139-60, where he writes of the NDE as involving temporal lobe activity.
34. Ibid., 134.
35. Morse, *Transformed*, 29; this question was italicized in the original.
36. Ibid., 67.
37. Ibid., 74.
38. Ibid., 89.
39. Ibid., 97.
40. Ibid., 61. Morse fails to stipulate just what a confirmed or validated psychic experience would be, thus leaving his claim a bit up in the air. Psychic experiences will be discussed in chapter 9.
41. Ibid., 236.
42. The nature of spiritual deception will be discussed in chapter 9.
43. Susan Blackmore, *Dying to Live: Near-Death Experiences* (Buffalo, NY: Prometheus Books, 1993), 111.
44. Susan Blackmore, *Beyond the Body: An Investigation of Out-of-Body Experiences* (London: Heinemann, 1982); quoted in Ian Wilson, *The After Death Experience* (New York: Morrow, 1987), 129.
45. Wilson, *After Death*, 129.
46. Ibid. This phenomenon is more akin to the autoscopic hallucination discussed in the Appendix, "Is It All in the Brain?"
47. Blackmore, *Dying*, 169.
48. Ibid., 173-82.
49. Ibid., 113-35.
50. This should not be confused with an autoscopic *hallucination*, which is discussed in the Appendix, "Is It All in the Brain?"
51. Sabom, *Recollections*, 86.
52. Ibid., 90.
53. Ibid., 91.
54. Ibid., 89.
55. Ibid., 104.
56. Ibid., 112-13.
57. Eadie, *Embraced*, 33-35.
58. Sabom, *Recollections*, 114.
59. Ibid.
60. Ibid.
61. Ibid., 106.
62. Ibid., 115.
63. Blackmore, *Dying*, 125.
64. Sabom, *Recollections*, 106.
65. Ibid., 105.
66. Ibid., 172.
67. Kenneth Ring and Madelaine Lawrence, "Further Evidence for Veridical Perception During Near-Death Experiences," *Journal of Near-Death Studies* 11 (Summer 1993): 226-27. In personal correspondence with me, Kenneth Ring reported some initial positive evidence for other corroborated OBEs, particularly with respect to OBEs in

the blind. A scholarly article on this should be forthcoming in the *Journal of Near-Death Studies*.

68. For more on the case for the existence of the soul and its immortality, see Gary R. Habermas and J.P. Moreland, *Immortality: The Other Side of Death* (Nashville, TN: Thomas Nelson, 1992); and Arthur C. Custance, *The Mysterious Matter of Mind* (Grand Rapids, MI: Zondervan Publishing House, 1980).

69. Ring has recently theorized as to the nature of negative NDEs, and has responded to comments on his views in the *Journal of Near-Death Studies* 13 (Fall 1994). This will be addressed in chapter 5.

70. Zaleski, *Otherworld*, 7.

Chapter 5—Near-Hell Experiences

1. Maurice Rawlings, *Beyond Death's Door* (1978; reprint, New York: Bantam Books, 1979), 3.

2. Ibid.

3. Ibid., 4.

4. Ibid.

5. Ibid., 5.

6. Raymond A. Moody, Jr., *Life After Life* (1975; reprint, New York: Bantam Books, 1976), 140.

7. Raymond A. Moody, Jr., *Reflections on Life After Life* (1977; reprint, New York: Bantam Books, 1978), 15.

8. Ibid., 18.

9. George G. Ritchie, *Return from Tomorrow* (Grand Rapids, MI: Fleming Revell, Baker Book House, 1978), 47-67. Ritchie's descriptions go beyond what is explicitly taught in the Bible.

10. Ibid., 67. Ritchie's testimony in *Return from Tomorrow* is essentially Christian. However, his later statements have not always agreed with biblical teachings.

11. P.M.H. Atwater, *Coming Back to Life: The After-Effects of the Near-Death Experience* (1988; reprint, New York: Ballantine Books, 1989), 15.

12. Ibid., 16.

13. Ibid. See also P.M.H. Atwater, *Beyond the Light: What Isn't Being Said About Near-Death Experience* (New York: Birch Lane Press, 1994), 35-36, for this account.

14. P.M.H. Atwater, "Is There a Hell? Surprising Observations About the Near-Death Experience," *Journal of Near-Death Studies* 10 (Spring 1992): 150.

15. Ibid., 149.

16. Ibid., 150.

17. Ibid.

18. Bruce Greyson and N.E. Bush, "Distressing Near-Death Experiences," *Psychiatry* 55:95-110.

19. Bruce Greyson, "Frightening NDEs Wanted for Research Study," *Vital Signs* III (Winter 1994): 4.

20. Atwater, "Is There a Hell?" 153.

21. Ibid., 154.

22. Ibid.

23. Atwater, *Beyond*, 43-45. Atwater deals with hell-like experiences on pages 27-45, which repeat much of what has been cited in the article above.

24. Charles A. Garfield, "The Dying Patient's Concern with 'Life After Death,'" in Robert Kastenbaum, ed., *Between Life and Death* (New York: Springer Publishing Company, 1979), 54.

25. Ibid., 55. Garfield may be including visions that did not involve clinical death. The article is not entirely clear on this.

26. The three categories of death will be discussed in chapter 7.

27. The Appendix, "Is It All in the Brain?" addresses the charge that NDEs are merely physical reactions in the dying brain and not spiritual experiences at all.

28. Kenneth Ring, *Life at Death: A Scientific Investigation of the Near-Death Experience* (New York: Coward, McCann, and Geoghegan, 1980), 194-95.

29. D. Scott Rogo, *Return from Silence: A Study of Near-Death Experiences* (England: The Aquarian Press, 1989), 136. Rogo is responding to Michael Sabom's review of Rawlings's book *Beyond Death's Door* (from *Anabiosis*, 1979, 1 (3), 9), and not to Ring himself; but his comments are applicable to Ring as well, since his position is very similar to Sabom's.

30. Rogo, *Return*, 136.

31. Margot Grey, *Return from Death*; quoted in Ibid., 139.

32. Rogo, *Return*, 141. See also Atwater, *Coming*, 18; and Greyson and Bush, "Distressing," 96.

33. Grey, *Return from Death*, 70; quoted in Sogyal Rinpoche, *The Tibetan Book of Living and Dying*, ed. Patrick Gaffrey and Andrew Harvey (San Francisco: HarperSanFrancisco, 1992), 329.

34. Grey, *Return from Death*; quoted in Rogo, *Return from Silence*, 142.

35. Ibid.

36. Ibid., 136-37.

37. Greyson and Bush, "Distressing," 109. See Carol Zaleski, *Otherworld Journeys: Accounts of Near-Death Experience in Medieval and Modern Times* (New York: Oxford Press, 1987), chapters 3-5 for medieval accounts of hell-like NDEs.

38. This is discussed in the Appendix, "Is It All in the Brain?"

39. Ring, *Life*, 248-49.

40. Kenneth Ring, "Solving the Riddle of Frightening Near-Death Experiences: Some Testable Hypotheses and a Perspective Based on *A Course in Miracles*," *Journal of Near-Death Studies* 13 (Fall 1994): 5-23; and Kenneth Ring, "Frightening Near-Death Experiences Revisited: A Commentary on Responses to My Paper by Christopher Bache and Nancy Evans Bush," in Ibid., 55-63.

41. Ring, "Frightening Near-Death Experiences," 59-61.

42. Ring, "Solving the Riddle," 15-16. For a critique of the channeled New Age document, *A Course in Miracles*, see Douglas Groothuis, *Revealing the New Age Jesus* (Downers Grove, IL: InterVarsity Press, 1990), 195-96, 198-202; and all the articles in *Spiritual Counterfeits Journal* 7, no. 1 (1987). In his explanation, Ring also considers the role of drugs and psychological mechanisms in negative NDEs, but he freely admits that his pantheistic, monistic viewpoint influences how he interprets the material.

43. Atwater, "Is There a Hell?" 160.

44. Atwater, *Coming*, 17.

45. Moody, *Reflections*, 36.

46. Ibid., 37.

47. We will deal with this in more detail in chapter 8.

48. On this see John W. Cooper, *Body, Soul, and Life Everlasting: Biblical Anthropology and the Monism-Dualism Debate* (Grand Rapids, MI: William B. Eerdmans Publishing Co., 1989), 143. W.G.T. Shedd nicely summarized the different statuses of the redeemed and the unredeemed after death: "The intermediate state [after physical death and before the resurrection of the body] for the saved is Heaven without the body, and the final state for the saved is Heaven with the body . . . the intermediate state for the lost is Hell without the body, and the final state is Hell with the body." W.G.T. Shedd, *The Doctrine of Endless Punishment* (New York: Scribner, 1886), 59-60; quoted in Gordon R. Lewis and Bruce A. Demarest, *Integrative Theology: Historical, Biblical, Systematic, Apologetic, Practical*, 3 volumes (Grand Rapids, MI: Zondervan, 1987-94) 3:473.

49. See Robert A. Morey, *Death and the Afterlife* (Minneapolis, MN: Bethany House Publishers, 1984), 147-49.

50. C.S. Lewis, *The Great Divorce* (1945), in *The Best of C.S. Lewis* (New York: Christianity Today, Inc., Iverson Associates, 1969), 111-12.

51. Jonathan Edwards, "The Justice of God in the Damnation of Sinners," in *Puritan Sage: Collected Writings of Jonathan Edwards*, ed. Vergilius Ferm (New York: Library Publishers, 1953), 294.

52. For more on the concept of "cosmic treason," see R.C. Sproul, *The Holiness of God* (Wheaton, IL: Tyndale House Publishers, 1985), 151.

53. Edwards, "The Justice of God," 294.

54. Moody, *Reflections*, 36.

55. For more on Isaiah's experience of the holy God, see Sproul, *Holiness*, 27-50.

56. Betty J. Eadie with Curtis Taylor, *Embraced by the Light* (Placerville, CA: Gold Leaf Press, 1992), 54-61.

57. Ibid., 72.

58. I owe this insight to Kenneth Myers who mentioned it to me in a conversation.

59. St. Gregory of Tours, *Dialogues* IV, 37, 237; quoted in Seraphim Rose, *The Soul After Death: Contemporary "After-Death" Experiences in the Light of the Orthodox Teaching on the Afterlife* (Platina, CA: Saint Herman of Alaska Brotherhood, 1980), 146.

60. Maurice Rawlings, *To Hell and Back: Life After Death, Startling New Evidence* (Nashville, TN: Thomas Nelson Publishers, 1992), 97.

61. Ibid., 76.

62. Personal interview with Dr. Mark Sheehan by Douglas Groothuis, December 1, 1994. This resuscitation occurred in April 1993 at Swedish Medical Center in Englewood, Colorado.

Chapter 6—Beliefs of the Near-Dead

1. Raymond A. Moody, Jr., with Paul Perry, *The Light Beyond* (New York: Bantam Books, 1988), 87-88.

2. Betty J. Eadie with Curtis Taylor, *Embraced by the Light* (Placerville, CA: Gold Leaf Press, 1992), 46.

3. Eadie's own religion, Mormonism, once taught this doctrine. See Richard Abanes, *"Embraced by the Light" and the Bible* (Camp Hill, PA: Horizon Books, 1994), 52-55.

4. John R.W. Stott, *Christ the Controversialist: A Study in Some Essentials of Evangelical Religion* (Downers Grove, IL: InterVarsity Press, 1970), 18.

5. Moody, *Light*, 39.

6. Ibid., 40.

7. Ibid., 88.

8. Ibid., 162-63. Ring's remarks are recorded by Moody, not quoted from another source, on pages 156-63.

9. Melvin Morse with Paul Perry, *Closer to the Light* (1990; reprint, New York: Ivy Books, 1991), 168.

10. Ibid., 168-69.

11. See John Ankerberg and John Weldon, *The Facts on Life After Death* (Eugene, OR: Harvest House, 1992), 20.

12. My view is that the loving choice is to conserve unborn human life, even in the face of difficulties, since this is the biblical position. My point here is that a fuzzy appeal to love is insufficient as a moral guide to behavior.

13. Stanislov Grof, book review of Kenneth Ring, *Heading Toward Omega: In Search of the Meaning of the Near-Death Experience* (1984), in *The Journal of Transpersonal Psychology* 16, no. 2 (1984): 246.

14. Joe Geraci, *Vital Signs*, December 1981, 12; quoted in Carol Zaleski, *Otherworld Journeys: Accounts of Near-Death Experience in Medieval and Modern Times* (New York: Oxford University Press, 1987), 126.

15. Dannion Brinkley with Paul Perry, *Saved by the Light* (New York: Villard Books, 1994), 20.

16. Ibid., 127.

17. Kenneth Ring, *Heading Toward Omega: In Search of the Meaning of the Near-Death Experience*, 2nd ed. (New York: Quill, 1985), 151.

18. Ibid.

19. P.M.H. Atwater, *Coming Back to Life: The After-Effects of the Near-Death Experience* (1988; reprint, New York: Ballantine Books, 1989), 155; emphasis in the original.

20. Ring, *Heading*, 57-58.

21. Melvin Morse with Paul Perry, *Transformed by the Light: The Powerful Effect of Near-Death Experiences on People's Lives* (1992; reprint, New York: Ivy Books, 1994), 79.

22. Ring, *Heading*, 87.

23. Ibid., 88.

24. Marilyn Ferguson, *The Aquarian Conspiracy* (Los Angeles: J.P. Tarcher, 1980), 87.

25. Ring, *Heading*, 220.

26. Eadie, *Embraced*, 81.

27. Ibid., 41.

28. Ibid., 71; emphasis in the original.

29. Ibid., 67; emphasis in the original.

30. For a theological and philosophical critique of pantheistic monism, see Douglas Groothuis, *Confronting the New Age: How to Resist a Growing Religious Movement* (Downers Grove, IL: InterVarsity Press, 1988), 106-26.

31. Ring, *Heading*, 62.

32. Ibid.

33. Eadie, *Embraced*, 70.

34. Raymond A. Moody, Jr., *Life After Life* (1975; reprint, New York: Bantam Books, 1976), 97-98.

35. Phillip Swihart, *The Edge of Death* (Downers Grove, IL: InterVarsity Press, 1978), 62-63.

36. Ring, *Heading*, 162.
37. For a discussion of the world's religions from a Christian viewpoint, see Harold Netland, *Dissonant Voices: Religious Pluralism and the Question of Truth* (Grand Rapids, MI: Eerdmans Publishing Company, 1991).
38. Ring, *Heading*, 162.
39. Morse, *Closer*, 141.
40. We will elaborate on this in chapter 8.
41. Ring, *Heading*, 159.
42. Atwater, *Coming*, 151.
43. P.M.H. Atwater, *Beyond the Light: What Isn't Being Said About Near-Death Experience* (New York: Birch Lane Press, 1994), 108.
44. Much more could be said about the unbiblical and illogical nature of reincarnation. See Douglas Groothuis, *Unmasking the New Age* (Downers Grove, IL: InterVarsity Press, 1986), 150-52; Douglas Groothuis, *Confronting the New Age* (Downers Grove, IL: InterVarsity Press, 1988), 85-103; Mark Albrecht, *Reincarnation: A New Age Teaching* (Downers Grove, IL: InterVarsity Press, 1987); Gary R. Habermas and J.P. Moreland, *Immortality: The Other Side of Death* (Nashville, TN: Thomas Nelson Publishers, 1992), 121-33.
45. Raymond Moody with Paul Perry, "Through the Looking Glass," *New Age Journal*, November/December 1993, 72. This article is an excerpt from Moody's book *Reunions: Visionary Encounters with Departed Loved Ones* (New York: Villard Books, 1993).
46. Ibid., 74-75.
47. For a fascinating account of the relationship of spiritism to permissive abortion, see Marvin Olasky, *Abortion Rites: A Social History of Abortion in America* (Wheaton, IL: Crossway Books, 1992), 61-82.
48. D. Scott Rogo, "Research on Deathbed Experiences," *Parapsychology Today*, January/February 1978, 21; cited in Ankerberg and Weldon, *The Facts on Life After Death*, 14.
49. See Robert A. Morey, *Death and the Afterlife* (Minneapolis, MN: Bethany House Publishers, 1984), 259-62.
50. As cited in Bernard J. Klamecki, "Medical Perspective of the Homosexual Issue," in J. Isamu Yamamoto, *The Crisis of Homosexuality* (USA: Victor Books, 1990), 126.
51. Maurice Rawlings, *Beyond Death's Door* (1978; reprint, New York: Bantam, 1979), 64.
52. Ibid.
53. Maurice Rawlings, *To Hell and Back: Life After Death, Startling New Evidence* (Nashville: Thomas Nelson Publishers, 1992), 54.
54. Moody, *Life*, 59.
55. Kenneth Ring's study of NDEs in *Life at Death: A Scientific Investigation of the Near-Death Experience* (New York: Coward, McCann, and Geoghegan, 1980), 188-89, did not find a being of light, but only light. See the discussion on Ring in chapter 4.
56. The dynamics of spiritual deception are addressed in chapter 9.
57. Ring, *Heading*, 112-14.
58. A.J. Ayer, "What I Saw When I Was Dead," in Terry Miethe and Anthony Flew, *Does God Exist? A Believer and an Atheist Debate* (San Francisco: HarperSanFrancisco, 1991), 225.
59. Ibid., 226. The legitimacy of this kind of physiological explanation of the NDE is discussed in the Appendix, "Is It All in the Mind?"

60. Ibid., 228.
61. Morse, *Closer*, 132.
62. Ibid., 184.
63. Ibid. It is curious that Morse transcribes these atheistic *interviews* by using a capital *L* in the word *Light*. This may suggest that he is reluctant to accept their atheistic interpretations.

Chapter 7—Do They Really Die?

1. Quoted in Pythia Peay, "Back from the Grave," *Utne Reader*, September/October 1991, 72; excerpted from *Common Boundary*, January/February 1991.
2. Michael Sabom, *Recollections at Death: A Medical Investigation* (New York: Harper and Row, 1982), 185. See the discussion of Sabom in chapter 4.
3. Raymond A. Moody, Jr., *Life After Life* (1975; reprint, New York: Bantam Books, 1976), 147.
4. Ibid., 150.
5. Sabom, *Recollections*, 8; Moody, *Life*, 146-47.
6. Moody, *Life*, 148.
7. Dina Ingber, "Visions of an Afterlife," *Science Digest*, January/February 1981, 97. Much to the disappointment of those researching NDEs, Dr. Shoonmaker has never published his findings.
8. Moody, *Life*, 150.
9. Sabom, *Recollections*, 8.
10. See 1 Kings 17:17-24; 2 Kings 4:8-37; Luke 7:11-17; John 11:1-44; Acts 20:7-12.
11. Moody, *Life*, 152.
12. This is discussed further in the Appendix, "Is It All in the Brain?"
13. P.M.H. Atwater, *Beyond the Light: What Isn't Being Said About Near-Death Experiences* (New York: Birch Lane Press, 1994), 83-95.
14. Ian Stevenson, Emily Williams Cook, Nicholas McClean-Rice, "Are Persons Reporting 'Near-Death Experiences' Really Near Death? A Study of Medical Records," *Omega* 20 (1989-90): 45.
15. Ibid., 53.
16. Ibid., 46.
17. Atwater, *Beyond*, 83.
18. Melvin Morse with Paul Perry, *Closer to the Light: Learning from the Near-Death Experiences of Children* (1990; reprint, New York: Ivy Books, 1991), 23. See the discussion of Morse in chapter 4.
19. George Gallup with William Proctor, *Adventures in Immortality* (New York: McGraw-Hill Book Company, 1982), 156.
20. Maurice Rawlings, *To Hell and Back* (Nashville, TN: Thomas Nelson Publishers, 1992), 10, says "from eight to eleven million Americans have already reported near-death experiences." This is most likely a wild overstatement.
21. Susan Blackmore, *Dying to Live: Near-Death Experiences* (Buffalo, NY: Prometheus Books, 1993), 32.
22. Ibid., 32-33.
23. Dannion Brinkley with Paul Perry, *Saved by the Light* (New York: Villard Books, 1994), 53-54, 60-61.
24. J.P. Moreland and Gary Habermas, *Immortality: The Other Side of Death* (Nashville: Thomas Nelson, 1992), 74; see also Sabom, *Recollections*, 185-86.

25. Sabom, *Recollections*, 185; emphasis in the original.
26. Moody, *Life*, 73-77.
27. Rawlings, *Beyond Death's Door* (1978; reprint, New York: Bantam Books, 1979), 46; and Melvin Morse with Paul Perry, *Transformed by the Light: The Powerful Effect of Near-Death Experiences on People's Lives* (New York: Ivy Books, 1992; reprint, 1994), 124.
28. P.M.H. Atwater, *Coming Back to Life: The After-Effects of the Near-Death Experience* (1988; reprint, New York: Ballantine Books, 1989), 180.
29. See Ian Wilson, *The After Death Experience* (New York: Quill, 1987), 129-30.
30. See Kerby Anderson, *Life, Death, and Beyond* (Grand Rapids, MI: Zondervan, 1980), 110-12.
31. Morse, *Closer*, 179.
32. Shirley MacLaine, *Out on a Limb* (New York: Bantam Books, 1983), 333.
33. See Kerby Anderson's discussion of these verses in *Life, Death, and Beyond*, 111-12. Nothing important is lost if these verses do not describe what some NDErs and OBErs report concerning a connecting cord. It is also important to remember that these verses do not endorse any occult activity that often accompanies NDEs and OBEs (Deuteronomy 18:10-12).
34. Hans Küng, *Eternal Life: Life After Death as a Medical, Philosophical, and Theological Problem* (Garden City, NY: Doubleday, 1984), 19-20.
35. I argue in chapter 8 that the ultimate reason to believe in life after death is the resurrection of Jesus Christ from the dead, who serves as the "first fruits" of a later resurrection (1 Corinthians 15:20-23).
36. Sogyal Rinpoche, *The Tibetan Book of Living and Dying* (San Francisco: HarperSanFrancisco, 1992), 331.
37. Moody, *Life*, 122.
38. A besetting difficulty in the Buddhist tradition is how to reconcile the dissolution of the personality at death with the idea that "something" from that person is reincarnated. What could be there to be reincarnated if the person is gone? To put it simply, you can't get someone from no one. On this issue see Paul J. Griffiths, *An Apology for Apologetics: A Study in the Logic of Interreligious Dialogue* (Maryknoll, NY: Orbis Books, 1991), 85-109.
39. For a discussion of this see Richard Leviton, "On Almost Hearing the Word of Return: Perspectives on the Near-Death Experience," *The Quest* 7 (Summer 1994): 79. This is a theosophical (occult and syncretistic) perspective.
40. Quoted in Ibid., 80.
41. *The Tibetan Book of the Dead*, ed. W.Y. Evans-Wenz (Oxford: Oxford University Press, 1960), 31; cited in Fr. Seraphim Rose, *The Soul After Death* (Platina, CA: Saint Herman of Alaska Brotherhood, 1980), 89.
42. Sabom, *Recollections*, 11.
43. As far as I know, as of this writing, January 1995.
44. Jim Jerome, "Heaven Can Wait," *People*, 11 October 1993, 81.
45. Interview with Hugh Downs, "20/20," ABC-TV, aired May 13, 1994.
46. Jerome, "Heaven," 81.
47. Ibid., 82.
48. Richard Abanes and Paul Carden, "A Special Report: What is Betty Eadie Hiding?" *Christian Research Journal* 16 (Winter 1994): 41.
49. Betty Eadie, "American Journal" program on KCAL, February 1994; quoted in Abanes, *"Embraced by the Light" and the Bible*, 203.

50. Betty J. Eadie with Curtis Taylor, *Embraced by the Light* (Placerville, CA: Gold Leaf Press, 1992), 25-28.
51. Ibid., 123-30.
52. Ibid., 133.
53. *The American Heritage Dictionary*, 3rd edition (Boston: Houghton Mifflin Company, 1992), 842.
54. The information presented here on standard post-surgical procedures in a case involving hemorrhage was supplied by Dr. Frank Knopp of Sevierville, Tennessee, a practicing obstetrician and gynecologist for 35 years, in an interview by Charles Strohmer, June 12, 1994.
55. Eadie, *Embraced*, 30.
56. Ibid., 123-25.
57. Ibid., 128-29.
58. Ibid., 129.
59. For more discussion of the veracity of Eadie's account of her death, see Abanes, "*Embraced by the Light*" *and the Bible*, 201-12.

Chapter 8—The Bible and the Near-Death Experience

1. Kenneth Ring, *Life at Death: A Scientific Investigation of the Near-Death Experience* (New York: Coward, McCann, and Geoghegan, 1980), 250.
2. George G. Ritchie, *Return from Tomorrow* (Grand Rapids, MI: Fleming H. Revell, Baker Book House, 1978), 15-16.
3. Maurice Rawlings, *To Hell and Back: Life After Death, Startling New Evidence* (Nashville, TN: Thomas Nelson Publishers, 1992), 62.
4. Ibid.
5. This way of putting it was suggested to me by John Ankerberg in a conversation.
6. Dannion Brinkley with Paul Perry, *Saved by the Light* (New York: Villard Books, 1994), 25.
7. For more on this, see the Appendix, "Is It All in the Brain?"
8. Phillip Swihart, *The Edge of Death* (Downers Grove, IL: InterVarsity Press, 1978), 47.
9. Raymond A. Moody, Jr., *Life After Life* (1975; reprint, New York: Bantam Books, 1976), 111.
10. Ibid., 113-14.
11. Ibid., 114.
12. Betty J. Eadie with Curtis Taylor, *Embraced by the Light* (Placerville, CA: Gold Leaf Press, 1992), 85.
13. Moody, *Life*, 112.
14. See the discussion of pantheistic monism in chapter 6.
15. Moody, *Life*, 115.
16. W. Harold Mare, commentary on 1 Corinthians in *The New International Study Bible*, Kenneth L. Barker, general editor (Grand Rapids, MI: Zondervan, 1985), 1757.
17. Raymond A. Moody, Jr., *Reflections on Life After Life* (1977; reprint, New York: Bantam Books, 1978), 65.
18. Melvin Morse, *Closer to the Light: Learning from the Near-Death Experiences of Children* (1990; reprint, New York: Ivy Books, 1991), 9.
19. Carol Zaleski, *Otherworld Journeys: Accounts of Near-Death Experience in Medieval and Modern Times* (New York: Oxford Press, 1987), 26-27.

20. Brinkley, *Saved*, 71.
21. Morse, *Closer*, 141.
22. Ibid., 142-43. For an understanding of what Jonathan Edwards really meant by a "divine light," see his essay "A Divine and Supernatural Light, Immediately Imparted to the Soul by the Spirit of God, Shown to Be Both a Scriptural and Rational Doctrine" in *Puritan Sage: Collected Writings of Jonathan Edwards*, ed. Vergilius Ferm (New York: Library Publishers, 1953), 157-63.
23. Some have been troubled by the speculations of the extremely liberal scholars who are part of the "Jesus Seminar" and who cast doubt on the historical reliability of much of the Gospels. Despite the media exposure that this group and their book *The Five Gospels: The Search for the Authentic Words of Jesus* (New York: Macmillan, 1993) have received, the Jesus Seminar's conclusions are neither new nor true. For a response to their claims, see D.A. Carson, "Five Gospels, No Christ," *Christianity Today*, 25 April 1994, 30-33; and Craig Blomberg, "The Seventy-Four 'Scholars': Who Does the Jesus Seminar Really Speak For?" *Christian Research Journal* 17 (Fall 1994): 32-40.
24. Gary R. Habermas and J.P. Moreland, *Immortality: The Other Side of Death* (Nashville, TN: Thomas Nelson Publishers, 1992), 69-72.
25. Edwin Yamauchi, "Easter—Myth, Hallucination, or History, Part Two," *Christianity Today*, 29 March 1974, 15ff.
26. Michael Green, *The Empty Cross of Jesus* (Downers Grove, IL: InterVarsity Press, 1984), 94.
27. Blaise Pascal, *Pensees*, trans. with introduction by A.J. Krailsheimer (New York: Penguin Books, 1966), #310/801, 125.
28. For more on the arguments for the resurrection, see Douglas Groothuis, *Revealing the New Age Jesus* (Downers Grove, IL: InterVarsity Press, 1990), 232-37; Habermas and Moreland, *Immortality*, 54-72; and, in more detail, William Lane Craig, *Knowing the Truth About the Resurrection* (Ann Arbor, MI: Servant Books, 1988).
29. C.S. Lewis, *Miracles* (New York: Macmillan Publishing Co., 1978), 145. The chapter from which this quote is taken, "Miracles of the New Creation," 143-63, is an excellent treatment of the implications and nature of Jesus' resurrection and of its effects on Christian believers.
30. For an excellent discussion of the importance of the doctrine of salvation (justification by faith) and its relationship to sanctification (growth as a Christian), see Richard F. Lovelace, *Dynamics of Spiritual Life: An Evangelical Theology of Renewal* (Downers Grove, IL: InterVarsity Press, 1979), 98-119.

Chapter 9—Psychic Powers

1. See John Ankerberg and John Weldon, *The Coming Darkness* (Eugene, OR: Harvest House Publishers, 1993), 51-59; and Douglas Groothuis, *Confronting the New Age: How to Resist a Growing Religious Movement* (Downers Grove, IL: InterVarsity Press, 1988), 25-26, 43-45.
2. Dannion Brinkley with Paul Perry, *Saved by the Light* (New York: Villard Books, 1994), 29-30.
3. Ibid., 31.
4. Raymond A. Moody, Jr., introduction to Brinkley, *Saved*, x-xi.
5. Ibid., 115.

6. Ibid., 119-20.
7. Melvin Morse with Paul Perry, *Transformed by the Light: The Powerful Effect of Near-Death Experiences on People's Lives* (1992; reprint, New York: Ivy Books, 1994), 104.
8. Ibid., 142-43.
9. P.M.H. Atwater, *Beyond the Light: What Isn't Being Said About Near-Death Experience* (New York: Birch Lane Press, 1994), 222.
10. Morse, *Transformed*, 91.
11. See Dan Korem, *Powers: Testing the Psychic and Supernatural* (Downers Grove, IL: InterVarsity Press, 1988); and James J. Randi, *The Magic of Uri Geller* (New York: Ballantine, 1975).
12. Kenneth Ring, *The Omega Project: Near-Death Experiences, UFO Encounters, and Mind at Large* (New York: William Morrow, 1992), 12.
13. Kenneth Ring, *Life at Death: A Scientific Investigation of the Near-Death Experience* (New York: Coward, McCann, and Geoghegan, 1980), 240.
14. Ibid., 241.
15. Kenneth Ring, "Near-Death and UFO Encounters as Shamanic Initiations: Some Conceptual and Evolutionary Implications," *ReVision* 11, no. 3: 19. For an analysis of Heraclitus's thought in relation to Eastern pantheistic monism, see R.C. Zaehner, *Our Savage God: The Perverse Use of Eastern Thought* (New York: Sheed and Ward, Inc., 1974), 74-103.
16. Ankerberg and Weldon, *Coming Darkness*, 31-49.
17. For a good summary of these ideas, see James Sire, *The Universe Next Door*, 2nd ed. (Downers Grove, IL: InterVarsity Press, 1988), 136-55.
18. Ring, *Omega Project*, 236.
19. Ibid., 215.
20. For an in-depth Christian critique of shamanism, see Brooks Alexander, "A Generation of Wizards: Shamanism and Contemporary Culture," *Spiritual Counterfeits Project: Special Collection Journal* 6 (Winter 1981): 24-29; and Brooks Alexander, "Shamanism in Two Cultures: Tantric Yoga in India and Tibet," in Ibid., 29-30.
21. Ring, *Heading Toward Omega: In Search of the Meaning of the Near-Death Experience*, 2nd ed. (New York: Quill, 1985), 230.
22. Ring, *Omega Project*, 164-72, 278-79.
23. Ibid., 165-66. For an analysis of the meaning of the modern UFO phenomenon and its relationship to spiritual beliefs, see William M. Alnor, *UFOs in the New Age: Extraterrestrial Messages and the Truth of Scripture* (Grand Rapids, MI: Baker Book House, 1992).
24. Bruce Greyson, "Scientific Commentary," in Barbara Harris and Lionel C. Bascom, *Full Circle: The Near Death Experience and Beyond* (New York: Pocket Books, 1990), 268.
25. Morse, *Transformed*, 100.
26. Ibid., 101.
27. See Ankerberg and Weldon, *Coming Darkness*; and Groothuis, *Confronting*, 76-83.
28. Ankerberg and Weldon, *Coming Darkness*, 147-58; Groothuis, *Confronting*, 77-79.
29. Bruce Greyson and Barbara Harris, "Counseling the Near-Death Experiencer," in *Spiritual Emergency: When Personal Transformation Becomes a Crisis*, eds. Stanislov Groff and Christina Groff (Los Angeles: J.P. Tarcher/Perigee, 1989), 201.
30. Ibid.
31. Morse, *Transformed*, 122.

32. Greyson and Harris, "Counseling," 204.

33. George Gallup, Jr., and George O'Connell, *Who Do Americans Say That I Am?* (Philadelphia: Westminster Press, 1986), 19.

34. Ibid.

35. George Barna, *Absolute Confusion: The Barna Report,* volume 3: 1993-94 (Ventura, CA: Regal Books, 1993), 272.

36. Gallup, *Who,* 62.

37. See chapter 8.

38. See chapter 8 for a discussion of the resurrection of Jesus.

39. On the differences between spiritual gifts and psychic powers, see Howard Ervin, *This Which Ye See and Hear* (Plainfield, NJ: Logos, 1972), 95-103.

40. For reasons to believe in the existence of a literal Satan, see Michael Green, *I Believe in Satan's Downfall* (Grand Rapids, MI: Eerdmans, 1981), 15-32; and Ankerberg and Weldon, *Coming Darkness,* 61-80. For a helpful perspective from a Christian counselor who encounters demonic phenomena, see Mark Bubeck, *Overcoming the Adversary* (Chicago, IL: Moody Press, 1984).

41. See the commentary by Robert Mounce in *The NIV Study Bible,* Kenneth Barker, ed. (Grand Rapids, MI: Zondervan Bible Publishers, 1985), 1926-27.

42. Eadie, *Embraced,* 41.

43. P.M.H. Atwater, *I Died Three Times* (Dayton, VA: n.p.), 22; quoted in Carol Zaleski, *Otherworld Journeys: Accounts of Near-Death Experience in Medieval and Modern Times* (New York: Oxford Press, 1987), 131.

44. Zaleski, *Otherworld,* 130.

45. Ibid., 128.

46. Raymond A. Moody, Jr., *Life After Life* (1975; reprint, New York: Bantam Books, 1976), 156.

47. St. Augustine, "The Divination of Demons," chapter 3 in *The Fathers of the Church,* volume 27, 426; quoted in Seraphim Rose, *The Soul After Death: Contemporary "After-Death" Experiences in the Light of the Orthodox Teaching on the Afterlife* (Platina, CA: Saint Herman of Alaska Brotherhood, 1980), 28-29.

48. Bishop Ignatius Brianchaninov, *Collected Works,* volume III, 19; quoted in Rose, *The Soul,* 58.

49. See Mark Albrecht and Brooks Alexander, "Thanatology: Death and Dying," *Journal of the Spiritual Counterfeits Project* 1 (April 1977): 6-7. For more background on Kubler-Ross and her occultic involvement, see Richard Abanes, *"Embraced by the Light" and the Bible* (Camphill, PA: Horizon Books, 1994), 147-58.

50. Robert E. Monroe, *Journeys Out of the Body* (Garden City, NY: Anchor, 1971) 138-39; quoted in J. Kerby Anderson, *Life, Death, and Beyond* (Grand Rapids, MI: Zondervan, 1980), 123-24. Anderson also notes that the spirit guide Seth of the *Seth Speaks* books, who was supposedly channeled by the late Jane Roberts, makes similar claims about spiritual transformations; see pages 124-25.

51. Sri Chinmoy, *Astrology, the Supernatural, and the Beyond* (Jamaica, NY: Agni Press, 1973), 62; and *Great Masters and Cosmic Gods* (Jamaica, NY: Agni Press, 1977), 8; cited in Ankerberg and Weldon, *Coming Darkness,* 148.

52. See Phillip J. Swihart, *The Edge of Death* (Downers Grove, IL: InterVarsity Press, 1978), 49-56.

53. Rose, *The Soul,* 102.

54. Ibid., 120; emphasis in the original.

55. Concerning the dangers of the occult in general, Ankerberg and Weldon, *Coming Darkness*, 26, warn that "the occult is hazardous because mankind's current status as spiritually, morally, and physically fallen does not properly equip him to deal safely with the realm of the supernatural. Ultimately, his knowledge of this world is miniscule, nor does he have the means to secure protection from whatever nasty things might exist there."

Chapter 10—Aftereffects
1. C.S. Lewis, *Letters to Malcolm: Chiefly on Prayer* (New York: Harcourt Brace Jovanovich, Inc., 1964), 80.

Appendix—Is It All in the Brain?
1. Melvin Morse, *Closer to the Light: Learning from the Near-Death Experiences of Children* (1990; reprint, New York: Ivy Books, 1991), 226.
2. Ibid., 214-15.
3. Ibid., 215.
4. Ibid., 216.
5. Ibid., 23.
6. Ibid., 218.
7. Raymond A. Moody, Jr., *Life After Life* (1975; reprint, New York: Bantam Books, 1976), 158-62.
8. Susan Blackmore, *Dying to Live: Near-Death Experiences* (Buffalo, NY: Prometheus Press, 1993), 41-45, argues that many elements of the NDE can occur through drugs like hashish and opium, but notes that NDEs still differ from drug-induced experiences in significant ways.
9. Morse, *Closer*, 218. Blackmore, *Dying*, 42, claims that ketamine can produce OBEs, but she doesn't specify if she includes autoscopic hallucinations in this category. But even if she refers to OBEs that are not autoscopic hallucinations, there remain differences between ketamine-induced OBEs and those occurring in NDEs.
10. Michael Sabom, *Recollections at Death: A Medical Investigation* (New York: Harper and Row, 1982), 165. See also Morse, *Closer*, 221-23; Moody, *Life*, 166-69; and Raymond A. Moody, Jr., *The Light Beyond* (New York: Bantam Books, 1988), 124-26.
11. Blackmore, *Dying*, 40.
12. Sabom, *Recollections*, 168-71.
13. Carol Zaleski, *Otherworld Journeys: Accounts of Near-Death Experience in Medieval and Modern Times* (New York: Oxford Press, 1987), 165.
14. Carl Sagan, *Broca's Brain* (New York: Ballantine Books, 1980), 356-57.
15. Blackmore *Dying*, 79-80
16. Ibid., 79-80.
17. Sabom, *Recollections*, 160-63.
18. Kenneth Ring, *Life at Death: A Scientific Investigation of the Near-Death Experience* (New York: Coward, McCann, and Geoghegan 1980), 207-08.
19. Sabom, *Recollections*, 167.
20. Ibid., 166; see also Ring, *Life* 208-10.
21. Moody, *Light*, 114
22. Ibid., 116-21.
23 Ibid., 121-24

24. Blackmore, *Dying*, 41-45.
25. Ibid., 49.
26. Ibid., 51.
27. Ibid.
28. Sabom, *Recollections*, 178.
29. Blackmore, *Dying*, 52. Morse, *Closer*, 224-25, makes a claim similar to Sabom's about the normalcy of blood oxygen levels in NDErs, but he does not specify how this was determined.
30. Ibid., 52.
31. Ibid., 65.
32. Ibid., 84.
33. Morse, *Closer*, 224.
34. Blackmore, *Dying*, 107.
35. Sabom, *Recollections*, 172.
36. Ibid.
37. Ibid.
38. Blackmore, *Dying*, 98-106.
39. Ibid., 214; and more generally, 202-25.
40. Ibid., 244-59.
41. This is discussed further in chapter 7.

OTHER GOOD
HARVEST HOUSE READING

THE BEAUTIFUL SIDE OF EVIL
by *Johanna Michaelsen*

Is there a beautiful side of evil? Is God *always* behind miracles? This is the true account of a woman who, searching for spiritual truth, became a personal assistant to a psychic surgeon. Then God revealed the true source behind the miraculous healings she witnessed. He lifted the veil of deception and allowed her to see the evil behind the outward appearance of beauty and holiness. Michaelsen reveals how this deadly deception is invading our lives.

THE COMING DARKNESS
by *John Ankerberg* and *John Weldon*

Millions of people are seeking the occult world and its alluring power. But this intriguing contact with supernatural power is not what it seems to be. Ankerberg and Weldon convincingly document with eyewitness accounts that occult practices are not "spiritual" or "godly." Rather, they are a deceptive trap backed by demonic power. The authors examine the history of occultism, look at reasons for the modern occult revival, provide an in-depth perspective on occult activity and its dangers, and then point the way to the source of *true* deliverance.

ANGELS AMONG US
by *Ron Rhodes*

Stories of angelic encounters are emerging all around us. So remarkable are some of these accounts that they have captured widespread attention. Curiously, however, many of these "celestial" visitors have little in common with the angels of the Bible. Angels *are* involved in our lives today—of that we can be certain. But when it comes to angels, how can we separate truth from fiction? Rhodes provides solid, biblically based answers to these questions and more by taking us on a fascinating—and inspirational—tour of God's Word. Discover who angels are, what they are like, what they do . . . and most exciting of all, the ministry they have in your life right now.

THE FACTS ON LIFE AFTER DEATH
by *John Ankerberg* and *John Weldon*

This 48-page booklet, part of "The Facts On" series, clearly shows how cults and parapsychology have modified the death experience. In this concise question-and-answer format, Ankerberg and Weldon address the cultic view of death, why near-death experiences frequently represent initiation into the world of the occult, the evidence for reincarnation, and much more.